TRANSATLANTIC
SLAVERY

AGAINST HUMAN DIGNITY

Edited by Anthony Tibbles

CLAIM
FOR THE COMPENSATION TO BE AWARDED FOR SLAVES.

Name of Estate, or Domicile of Slaves.	BRITISH GUIANA.	No.
Good Intent	District of Demerary & Essequebo.	

THE CLAIM of *William King Esq. of New Amsterdam as Executor of William Searles, dec.d — owner in fee &c*

in the Parish of *St John —*

by George Warren his Attorney

to the COMPENSATION for *One hundred and three* SL

in the possession of the said *William King —*

on the 1st of August, 1834, duly registered, [except as undermentioned,] and de

in the Return made thereof, on the   day of

Geo. Warren JY

Number of Slaves Registered 31st May, 1832....... *One hund*

sixteen

Alterations from 31st May, 1832, to 1st August, 1834.   *11*

INCREASE BY BIRTH.

Sex.	Name.	Age.	Mother's Name.	
Male	*Tom*	*14 Months*	*Rose*	
"	*Melville*	*10 "*	*Leonora*	*2*

TRANSATLANTIC
SLAVERY

AGAINST HUMAN DIGNITY

Edited by Anthony Tibbles

LIVERPOOL
UNIVERSITY PRESS

NATIONAL MUSEUMS LIVERPOOL

Published by:
National Museums Liverpool
William Brown Street
Liverpool L3 8EL

Liverpool University Press
4 Cambridge Street
Liverpool L69 7ZU

This catalogue was first published to accompany the opening of the Transatlantic Slavery Gallery at Merseyside Maritime Museum in Liverpool. The Gallery was initiated and has been generously sponsored by the Peter Moores Foundation.

ISBN 0-85323-198-2

First published in 1994
This edition © National Museums Liverpool 2005

British Library Cataloguing in Publication Data
A CIP catalogue record for this book is available from the British Library

Designed by DL and AW www.axisgraphicdesign.co.uk
Printed by Compass Press

Contents

Foreword

DAVID FLEMING

Director, National Museums Liverpool

I am privileged to write this foreword to the second edition of this important book. In the first edition my distinguished predecessor as Director of National Museums Liverpool, Sir Richard Foster, noted that the project to create Liverpool's Transatlantic Slavery Gallery in 1994 had been 'challenging', and indeed it was so. Many people were involved in bringing that project to life, and millions have since viewed, and marvelled, and despaired at the story told in that Gallery.

This is the power of museums – they can reach out to audiences, and touch them in a way no book can. And yet museum displays are ephemeral. Unlike books they do not go on forever. They change, sometimes they disappear altogether, replaced by a display on another subject. But that is not to be the fate of the Transatlantic Slavery Gallery. It is changing, yes, but it is getting bigger, and it will tell yet more stories about the horrors of the transatlantic slave trade and its legacies.

Indeed, in 2007 National Museums Liverpool intend to launch a new national museum, the National Museum of Transatlantic Slavery, the running costs of which will be met by the British Government. It is in looking forward to this new museum that the new edition of this publication is produced. The two projects – book and museum – go hand in hand. Both attempt to explain, for an almost disbelieving audience, how and why such an inhuman trade could be conducted by a supposedly civilized Western culture, over such a long period.

It is appropriate that this story is related in Liverpool, a city which was once the slaving capital of the world, raised to a stupendous level of prosperity through the profits of trading in enslaved African men, women and children. It is also appropriate that the new museum – only metres away from the eighteenth century dry docks where slaving ships were actually repaired – opens in 2007, the bi-centenary of the abolition of the British slave trade though not, alas, the end of slave trading or slavery.

Thanks are due to all the contributors to this book, to all those who created the Transatlantic Slavery Gallery, and to all those who are creating the new museum. This is a story which must be told, and we must not heed those who believe it should be consigned to the history books. The legacy of this horrendous trade lives on, in racism and intolerance, in the plight of Africa and many other people of African descent, and in the rich cultures of African, African Caribbean, African American, and African European people. One of the more extraordinary aspects of the slave trade, indeed, is the resilience of African cultures even when torn forcibly from their homelands, and the impact and influence they have had on other cultures.

If, through the impact of this book, and through the power of the National Museum of Transatlantic Slavery, we make a contribution to harmony and understanding between peoples from different backgrounds, and help counter racism and racial intolerance, then our efforts will have been worthwhile.

Advisory Committee and Curators

Advisory Committee
Lord Pitt of Hampstead, Chairman

Dame Jocelyn Barrow

Wally Brown (to July 1993)

Angus Chukuemeka

Alissandra Cummins

Richard Foster

Len Garrison

Professor Stuart Hall

Herbie Higgins

Professor Alistair Hennessy

Barbara Johnstone

Professor Preston King

Dorothy Kuya

Sir Shridath Ramphal

Dr Stephen Small

Sir Kenneth Stuart

Alan Swerdlow

Sir David Wilson

Guest Curators' Group
Femi Biko, Lecturer, Lambeth Education Institute, London

Allisandra Cummins, Director, Barbados Museum and Historical Society

Dr Mary E. Modupe Kolawole, Senior Lecturer, African Women's Cultural and Literary Studies, Obafemi Awolowo University, Ile-Ife, Nigeria

Preston King, Professor of Political Philosophy, Lancaster University

Paul Lovejoy, Professor, Department of History, York University, Ontario, Canada

Patrick Manning, Professor, Department of African-American Studies, Northwestern University, Boston, USA

Jennifer Morgan, Research Fellow, University of South Carolina, USA

Edward Reynolds, Professor of History, University of California, San Diego, USA

David Richardson, Reader in Economic History, University of Hull

Dr Stephen Small, Lecturer in Sociology, University of Leicester

James Walvin, Professor of History, University of York

NMGM project/curatorial team
Anthony Tibbles, Curator of Maritime History and Project Leader

Alison Taubman, Project Curator

Gail Cameron, Assistant Curator (to August 1993)

Joanne Howdle, Assistant Curator (from November 1993)

Garry Morris, Project Outreach Worker

Paul Rees, Senior Education Officer

Keith Robinson, Senior Designer

Edmund Southworth, Curator of Archaeology & Ethnology

Sally-Ann Yates, Project Co-ordinator for Conservation Division

Consultant Designer
Ivor Heal Design Ltd

Foreword to First Edition

SIR PETER MOORES

Patron, Peter Moores Foundation

During forty years of work and travel in Europe and America, it became increasingly clear to me that slavery was a taboo subject, both to white and to black people. Forty years ago, most Europeans had managed to suppress any acknowledgement of their connection with the slave trade. It was something in the past. In the United States, where it was impossible to ignore the results of the slave trade, there was segregation, later bussing and recently something like integration, but never any mention of how black people came to be in America in the first place. We can come to terms with our past only by accepting it, and in order to be able to accept it we need knowledge of what actually happened. We need to make sense of our history.

It seemed to me that the taboo should be exorcised, and black friends agreed with me. I am pleased that my idea to have a permanent slave trade gallery has been taken up by National Museums and Galleries on Merseyside. It is particularly appropriate that this gallery should be in Liverpool, which not only has one of the oldest black communities in Europe but was also the major European slaving port in the eighteenth century.

A visit to the exhibition is bound to disturb us – black or white. But it is meant to bring the slave trade before us without mincing matters, to act as a catalyst which will spark off reflection, debate, understanding and further study.

During the two years leading up to the opening of the gallery, a distinguished group of people from Liverpool and around the world have worked together to research, debate, advise and guide the project in the right direction. I am grateful for the support which they have given and feel privileged to be associated with these enthusiastic, dedicated and committed people whose work has made this exhibition possible.

Introduction

ANTHONY TIBBLES

In the period between about 1500 and about 1870, millions of Africans were enslaved and transported across the Atlantic by Europeans, who needed a labour force to develop and work in their American colonies. Although this is usually described as the 'Atlantic Slave Trade', we have chosen to adopt the wider, more embracing term 'Transatlantic Slavery' as the title for the gallery, not least because 'slave trade' concentrates on the dehumanizing aspects. We have to be able to see beyond the mechanics of the operation and remember that this is a story about people.

The system of transatlantic slavery is often referred to as the Triangular Trade. Seen from this perspective, there were three stages, involving the three continents of Europe, Africa and America. Ships set out from ports on the western seaboard of Europe – from Spain, Portugal, the Netherlands, England, France and even Denmark and Sweden – laden with a variety of trade goods. Arriving on the west coast of Africa, captains exchanged these goods for enslaved Africans. The process often took weeks or months. The second leg of the journey was the infamous 'Middle Passage' from Africa across the Atlantic. On arrival the captives who had survived the voyage were sold and put to work. The final stage of the trade saw the ships returning to Europe with goods, in particular sugar, coffee, tobacco and rice, or with credit notes. The merchants and their investors then took their profits, which supported their lifestyle or were reinvested in property, land and other new ventures.

But it is not accurate to see the system as always taking a triangular form. There were, for instance, a significant number of bi-lateral voyages between Brazil and Africa, particularly after the official abolition of the trade in the nineteenth century. Nor should it be forgotten that the direct trade between Europe and its American colonies in the seventeenth and eighteenth centuries was equally dependent on slavery. The goods brought back were produced by slave labour, which was sustained by the trade in Africans.

Of course, for the Africans, the experience was very different. For many of those enslaved the process began away from the coast as they were seized in wars or raids and were sold from one trader to another. They often faced long arduous journeys and few knew what final destination or fate awaited them. On arrival at the coast they were usually imprisoned in forts before being loaded on to ships. Few would have ever seen the sea, or a ship, or a white man before. They found themselves thrown together with people from different parts of Africa, speaking different languages, in conditions of horror, deprivation and violence. In this way they crossed the Atlantic. On arrival in the Americas, they were parted from their shipmates and often their families as they were sold to different owners. Many faced further journeys as they were led to the plantations and other places where they were put to work. The vast majority knew only a life of hard labour ending in death far from home.

The essays which follow are not intended to provide a blow-by-blow account of transatlantic slavery. Most are adaptations of briefing papers prepared for the gallery. They do, however, address many of the key issues involved. Some look at specific topics, some are broader. Some are a synthesis of current research, others adopt a more personal approach. It is my hope that they will cause people to think about transatlantic slavery, to understand the context and to recognize that it has relevance for all of us today.

Note to Second Edition

Although published more than a decade ago, the essays in this book have stood the test of time well and they still provide an excellent introduction to the subject of transatlantic slavery. In preparing this second edition, we have taken the opportunity to include two extra articles. The first is Lonnie Bunch's 'The Challenge of Remembering Slavery', which was presented at the Merseyside Maritime Museum as the first International Slavery Day Lecture in August 2003. NML has championed UNESCO's International Day for the Remembrance of the Slave Trade and its Abolition on 23 August each year since 1999. This paper succinctly summarizes why the issues of transatlantic slavery are so important today. The second article examines the role of museums in the public interpretation of transatlantic slavery and particularly the contributions made in recent years. It takes as its focus the development of NML's Transatlantic Slavery Gallery and its impact in encouraging museums to address issues related to this important subject.

55
Trade Token, inscribed 'Tom Buck of Granny Bonny, an Honest Trader ...'
Ivory

30
Map of Europe and North Africa
Parchment, 16th century

The Rise of the
Atlantic Empires

DAVID RICHARDSON

The fifteenth and sixteenth centuries are often described as the 'Age of Discoveries'. Helped by improvements in maritime technology, Portuguese navigators explored the west coast of Africa in the fifteenth century, colonizing before 1480 the Atlantic islands of Azores, Madeira and Cape Verde as well as Sao Tome in West Africa. A trading station was then established at El Mina on the Gold Coast of Africa in 1481, before further voyages took the Portuguese into the Indian Ocean after 1498 and across the Atlantic to Brazil in the early sixteenth century. By this date, however, the Genoese-born Columbus had already made three voyages on behalf of the Spanish crown to the West Indies, and from there Spanish interest soon spread to the mainland. Victories by Cortes over the Aztecs in 1521 and by Pizarro over the Incas a decade later helped to create a Spanish empire in the Americas that, by 1550, stretched from Mexico in the north to Bolivia in the south and included Hispaniola and Cuba in the Caribbean.

The voyages that led to the Portuguese and Spanish empires were mainly intended to develop sea-routes to the East, thus removing Europe's dependence on Middle-Eastern Muslim traders for supplies of spices and other Eastern luxuries. However, their Atlantic empires became major sources of wealth for Portugal and Spain in their own right. In both cases, initial efforts to develop production in their Atlantic colonies centred on sugar. Under Venetian and Genoese influence this crop had become widely cultivated throughout the Mediterranean after its discovery by Europeans in the Middle East at the time of the Crusades. However, sugar cane requires all-year-round heat and moisture and growing conditions in the Mediterranean were less than ideal. Better conditions were to be found in Madeira, the Canaries, Sao Tome, the

West Indies and Brazil, and this encouraged the Portuguese and Spanish, with Italian financial support, to attempt sugar cultivation there. Production began at Madeira in the 1450s and, by 1500, was also under way at Sao Tome and Hispaniola. Spanish interest in sugar cultivation in the Americas diminished, however, in the early sixteenth century as gold and silver began to flow after the 1520s from mines in Peru and Bolivia. And until the establishment of sugar and coffee cultivation in Cuba and Puerto Rico in the late eighteenth century, silver dominated exports from Spanish America. However, sugar production in the Portuguese empire spread from the Atlantic islands to Brazil during the 1540s and grew rapidly during the following century. Averaging 20–30,000 tons a year, Brazilian sugar exports dominated the European market by the 1630s, squeezing out Madeiran and Mediterranean suppliers and totally overshadowing sugar production in the West Indies. In the sixteenth and seventeenth centuries sugar dominated the Portuguese Atlantic empire as much as silver dominated the Spanish.

Under the Treaty of Tordesillas, signed in June 1494, Portugal and Spain had sought to divide up the world outside Europe, Spain claiming all land west of a line 370 leagues beyond the Cape Verde islands, and Portugal all land east of this line. Ceding Africa and the then unknown Brazil to Portugal, the treaty handed the rest of the Americas to Spain. The limited administrative and financial resources of the two Catholic powers combined with rivalry between Spain and France in Europe and the rise of Protestant powers such as England and Holland to ensure that Portugal and Spain had little chance of enforcing their monopoly of the extra-European world. Portugal's proposed monopoly on trade to Africa,

6
Scorpion
Gold, Central South America

1
Part of beaker with face
Silver, Peru

for instance, was broken in the 1530s by the French and later by the English adventurers Thomas Wyndham and John Hawkins. Wyndham made three voyages to Morocco and West Africa in 1551–53 while Hawkins made three voyages to Sierra Leone in 1562–69, carrying off some 1,200 Africans into slavery. Later, in 1580, Portugal lost its independence to Spain and before re-establishing it in 1640 saw the Dutch gain control in the 1630s of Portuguese territories in Angola and Brazil.

Despite their superior resources, the Spanish fared no better than the Portuguese in maintaining their monopoly of dealings with the rest of the Americas. Among those infringing Spanish claims was John Hawkins, who sold the slaves he had taken from Sierra Leone in the 1560s at Hispaniola. And he was followed in the final years of the century by his kinsman, Francis Drake, who made four raids on the Spanish Caribbean between 1570 and 1596. Turning Hawkins and Drake into Elizabethan heroes, these ventures depended on support from the state as well as London's merchant community. Converting private capital into an instrument of the state, they demonstrated how, in the following century, England, Holland and France would create their own formal transatlantic empires. England founded its first colony at Virginia in 1607. Then in the 1620s it added Barbados and the Leeward Islands in the West Indies and began to extend its mainland empire northward to New England and southward into Maryland before seizing Jamaica from Spain in 1655. At the same time, trading factories were established in West Africa at Cormantin (1631) and Cape Coast (1649) on the Gold Coast and James Fort on the Gambia (1661).

While English merchants, courtiers and adventurers were establishing Britain's first colonial empire, their counterparts in France and Holland were creating theirs. Achieving independence from Spain in 1609, the Dutch temporarily seized north-eastern Brazil and Angola in 1629–30 before gaining more permanent possession of Curacao (1634), St Eustatius (1635) and Surinam (1667) in the West Indies as well as trading stations such as El Mina (1637) in Africa. Similarly the French settled Guadaloupe and Martinique in 1635, established trading stations in the vicinity of Senegal in the 1670s, and in 1697 formally annexed the greatest prize of all, St Domingue, the western part of Hispaniola.

Thus during the course of the seventeenth century, England, Holland and France had joined Portugal and Spain as major imperial powers in the Atlantic world. Their colonies provided bases from which to acquire through trade or other means the silver and other riches of Spanish America. Colonization involved, however, significant investment by courtiers and merchants, and from the outset, the founders of most colonies sought to develop cash crops or other goods for export to Europe in order to secure a return on their investments. By 1620, Virginia had begun to produce tobacco for export, and over the following 150 years this became the staple export of the colony as well as of its neighbour, Maryland. Cultivation of tobacco and some other crops was also tried for a time in some of the West Indian islands, but during the mid-1640s sugar cane was introduced to Barbados by Dutch merchants and planters following the expulsion from Brazil by the Portuguese. By 1680 the crop had transformed the island into 'the richest colony in English America'. From Barbados sugar cultivation spread rapidly to the English Leeward Islands and French Martinique and Guadaloupe and then to Jamaica and St Domingue in the early eighteenth century and the Spanish West Indies, especially Cuba, a little later.

Sugar was not, however, the only export from the 'sugar' colonies. Brazil itself experienced a gold boom in 1680–1750 as well as a coffee boom in the nineteenth century, while dye stuffs such as logwood and pimento, ginger, cotton, cocoa and coffee emerged as significant exports from the West Indies between 1660 and 1850. The foundation and development of other colonies outside Brazil and the Caribbean added to the diversification of colonial goods entering transatlantic trade after 1660. Fish, furs and forest products became significant exports from Newfoundland, Quebec and other colonies north of Virginia, while rice and indigo emerged as major exports from the Carolinas in the eighteenth century. In addition, from 1790 cotton became a key export from the southern states of the newly established U.S.A., rapidly displacing cotton exports from the West Indies. Despite these developments, precious metals from South America and sugar from Brazil and the West Indies remained the cornerstones of trade from America to Europe until well into the nineteenth century.

The exact scale of such trades can never be determined, but it is estimated[1] that between 1500 and 1800 as much as 100,000 metric tonnes of silver and 2,500 tonnes of gold were produced in South America, with over half being produced during the Mexican silver and Brazilian gold booms of the eighteenth century. Figures for sugar[2] suggest

7
Idol, two male figures joined at body
Tumbaga, Mexico

9
Funerary mask with repoussé facial features
Tumbaga, with vestiges of red paint, Sican culture, Peru, c.900–1500

that annual exports from the Americas to Europe rose from about 30,000 metric tonnes in 1650 to almost 200,000 tonnes in the mid-eighteenth century and to 900,000 tonnes a century later. Brazil dominated the trade before 1650, Jamaica and St Domingue in the eighteenth century, and Cuba, Puerto Rico, Guyana and a revitalized Brazil in the nineteenth century.

Expanding production and export of precious metals and sugar depended on several factors. These included improvements in ocean-going shipping and navigational skills in Europe, the transfer across the Atlantic of European capital, commercial practices and mining and agricultural technologies, and the seizure by European colonists of property rights over land in America from the indigenous population. The last was achieved largely through military conquest and the elimination, partly through violence but mainly through disease, of many of the indigenous peoples of the Americas. Throughout America, contact with Europeans and exposure to the diseases which they carried led to catastrophic declines in local populations, with some peoples, including the Arawaks and Caribs of the West Indies, disappearing completely.

While such demographic catastrophes facilitated the transfer of rights to land to Europeans, they also deprived the colonists of a potential source of labour with which to exploit the land and to earn a profit from it. In most colonies, attempts were made initially to enslave the Indian population, but local resistance to such practices as well as population decline invariably led to their abandonment in favour of recruiting labour from other sources. In the colonies north of Virginia, white labour became the basis of long-term development. Furthermore, the growth of tobacco output in Virginia and Maryland in the seventeenth century also depended heavily on white labour, mainly in the form of indentured servants or convict labour. The former normally worked for four to five years for those who paid for their passage from Europe, while convicts often faced fourteen years of forced labour in the colonies. From their earliest days of colonial expansion, however,

2
Beaker, repoussé decoration of bands with scrolls and birds
Silver, Peru

4
Figurine
Tumbaga, Columbia

10
Duho
Carved wood, Taino, Caribbean

Fig.1
Spaniards attacking the Aztec city of Tenochtitlan, 1519,
from The Florentine Codex, Spanish, early 16th century.

the Portuguese and Spanish had turned primarily to enslaved Africans to work their American lands. And when the western European powers began to create and develop their empires in America, they quickly followed the lead given by the Iberian powers.

In retrospect, this seems hardly surprising, for the trans-Saharan slave trade had, by the fifteenth century, long supplied enslaved labour from Africa to work alongside white slaves from Russia and the Balkans on the sugar plantations of the Mediterranean. And with the charting of the west coast of Africa by Portugal in the fifteenth century, an easy supply of controllable labour opened up to the Portuguese to work the sugar plantations they were seeking to establish at Madeira and Sao Tome. Inextricably linking African slaves to European colonial expansion, developments in the Portuguese Atlantic islands in 1450–1500 foreshadowed the pattern of socio-economic development in Spanish America, Brazil, the West Indies and the southern colonies of North America. Over the following four centuries, forced African labour was combined with European capital to exploit the lands and natural resources of the Americas. Thus, the eighteenth-century writer, Malachy Postlethwayt, rightly claimed that the African slave trade was 'the Great Pillar and Support' of British trade with America and that the British empire was 'a magnificent superstructure of American commerce and [British] naval power on an African foundation'.[3] Although related to Britain's empire, Postlethwayt's remarks were equally applicable to the American empires of Portugal, Spain, France and Holland between 1500 and 1850.

Notes

1   Ward Barrett, 'World Bullion Flows, 1450–1900' in J. D. Tracy (ed.), *The Rise of Merchant Empires: Long-Distance Trade in the Early Modern World 1350–1750*, Cambridge 1990.
2   Noel Deerr, *The History of Sugar*, 2 vols, London 1949–50.
3   Malachy Postlethwayt, *The African Trade, The Great Pillar and Support of the British Plantation Trade in America*, London 1745.

Fig.2
Caribs attacking the crew of a British ship on St Lucia, 1608, from *Historia Americae* by Theodore Bry, published Frankfurt, 1634. The Caribs were one of the indigenous peoples of the Caribbean. They were enslaved, murdered or died from diseases which Europeans brought with them.

106

Map of the Virgin Islands, printed coloured chart
Thomas Jefferys, London, 1775

100

Chart of the Caribbean and Gulf of Mexico, printed and coloured
Nicolas Visscher, Amsterdam, c.1700

110
Map of St Lucia, printed chart with insets of Carenage, Cul de Sac des Roseaux and Grand Islet
Jacques Nicolas Bellin, Paris 1763

107
Map of Curacao, printed chart with plan, elevation and six views
Gerard van Keulen, Amsterdam, 1st quarter 18th century

Human Cargoes: Enslavement and the Middle Passage

EDWARD REYNOLDS

When the Portuguese started to sail down the African coast in the early decades of the fifteenth century, they were aware of the commercial possibilities that the continent offered. They saw opportunities to exploit rich fishing banks and extract quantities of gold from the African peoples. At the same time, the prospect of capturing and selling Africans was not lost upon them. It was the Portuguese who began to capture Africans for export.

In 1441 Antam Goncalves, a Portuguese sailor, seized ten Africans near Cape Bojador. Cited frequently as the beginning of the Atlantic slave trade, this event in 1441 was not formal trade but kidnapping. This type of kidnapping could not be sustained for a long period without retribution from Africans and it later yielded to a formal trade between Africans and Europeans.

Most of the slaves sold to Europeans were acquired through wars and raids. Wars and raids are lumped together because what were often called wars were in fact slave raids. Wars to acquire slaves expanded as the external demand increased. Wars which led to the acquisition of slaves were often motivated by economic gain and African chiefs often weighed the odds of winning and obtaining these benefits before embarking upon such wars. European slave traders encouraged wars through the sale of guns and gunpowder. They were active participants in the wars and conflicts that produced slaves. A slave-ship captain wrote: 'I verily believe, that the far greater part of the wars in Africa, would cease, if the Europeans would cease to tempt them with goods for slaves'. In 1703 the Dutch West Indian Company trading on the Gold Coast supplied the state of Akwamu with one hundred soldiers and firearms to wage war against their neighbours with the resultant slaves going to the Dutch. Warfare for slaves encouraged retaliation and set off a cycle of violence.

Slaves were also kidnapped. Kidnapping was nothing more than stealing a person and, like warfare and raiding, it introduced considerable violence into the society. Unwary individuals, especially women and children, when found alone in isolated places were easy prey for kidnappers.

According to a trader: '... an Abundance of little blacks of both sexes were stolen away by their neighbours, when found on roads in the wood'. Such acts of violence no doubt affected trading and other peaceful occupational activities.

Indebtedness led to slavery. When individuals incurred debts and were unable to repay the loans, they were sold into slavery. Even individuals who had been given as pawns (pledges) for debts were not always free from seizure. Slaves were received as tribute by strong states. An area of great misunderstanding is enslavement through the 'judicial process'. Individuals were condemned to slavery for alleged crimes, and by the seventeenth century the laws of some societies functioned as a handmaiden to the trade. A traveller reported that: 'The Kings are so absolute, that upon any slight pretense of offense committed by their subjects, they order them to be sold for slaves without regard to rank or profession'. Another traveller wrote: 'some of the negroe rulers, corrupted by the Europeans, violently infringe the law of Guinea'. Other infractions that led to enslavement included the practice of witchcraft and the violation of taboos in the society. But the way the 'law' was applied provided room for fraud. Many Africans who were enslaved were not criminals and had violated no laws.

Whatever the method of enslavement, the slaves were marched down from the interior to the forts and factories on the coast that were staffed by Europeans. The slaves arrived in dejected and exhausted condition at the coast, where they were sold through African brokers.

56
Trade token
Ivory

Fig.3
Slave and traders, Sierra Leone, 1682, from O.F. von der Groben,
Guineische Reise, 1694. A Portuguese merchant (right) is shown
trading for slaves and ivory.

Before Europeans could start trading and buying the slaves, it was customary for them to pay duties and give gifts to the African rulers on the coast. After this exchange of gifts, the slaves were carefully examined from head to toe, without regard to sex, to see that they did not have any blemishes or defects. Some of the slaves were rejected if defects were identified. Among the slavers was a clear preference for fifteen- to twenty-five-year-old males, who represented about two thirds of the slaves.

Most Africans understandably showed extreme levels of distress and despair at being torn away from their homeland, and dreaded what came to be known as the Middle Passage. Some feared that they were being taken away to be eaten by their captors; the attempts by some slavers to explain to the victims the purpose for which they had been purchased failed to allay their fears. Thus some slaves resisted being put on board the slave ships and even tried to drown themselves as they were being taken to the ships.

The conditions on slave ships were slovenly and foul. The height of the decks averaged between four and five feet. In addition to the slave holds, some slavers built half-decks along the sides of the ships, extending no farther than the sides of the scuttles, where slaves, lying in two rows, one above the other, were crowded together and were fastened by leg-irons. Slaves were brought upon deck at mid-morning and those who had died during the night were thrown into the ocean. The slaves were given water with which to wash, and the ship's surgeon then examined them for sores and other ailments. Meals were served twice daily: breakfast at mid-morning and the other meal late in the afternoon.

To control the hungry captives' food consumption, the process of eating was sometimes directed by signals from a monitor, who indicated when the slaves should dip their fingers or wooden spoons into the food and when they should swallow. It was the responsibility of the monitor to report those who refused to eat, and any slaves found to be attempting to starve themselves were severely whipped. According to a ship's surgeon, 'Upon the negroes refusing to take sustenance I have seen coals of fire, glowing hot, put on a shovel, and placed so near their lips as to scorch and burn them'. The surgeon continued, 'And this has been accompanied with threats, of forcing them to swallow the coals, if they any longer persisted in refusing to eat'. At other times, the *speculum orum*, a mouth opener, was used to force-feed the slaves.

Log books were kept on the ship's provisions. These records were vital, since the vessel's capacity did not allow

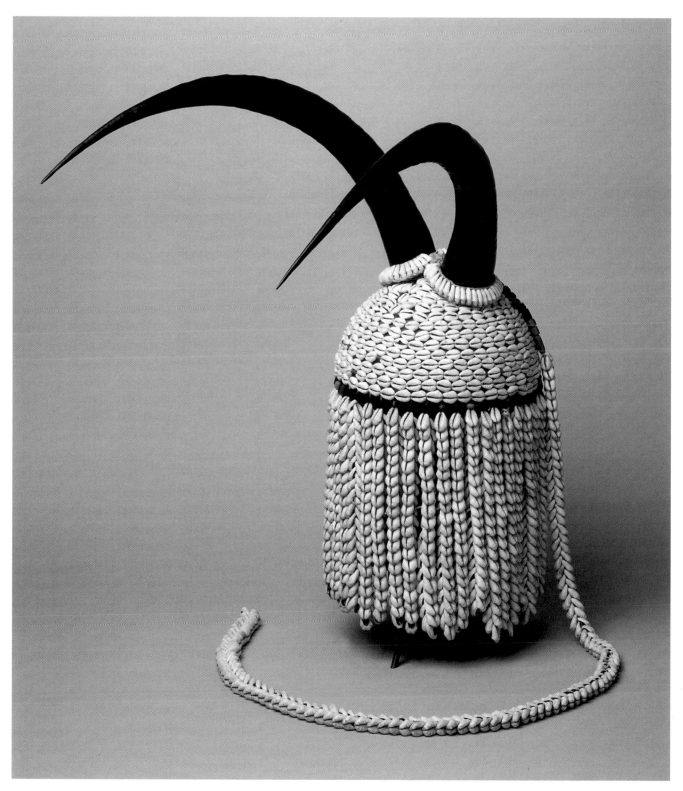

58
Head-dress of cowrie shells with roan antelope horns
Kon Kombo, West Africa

59
String of cowrie shells
West Africa

60
Necklace
Hollow tubes of coiled wires, brass
Muni River, Eloby, West Africa

98
Surgical instrument set
London, late 18th/early 19th century

73
Four Queen Manillas
Copper

for emergency provisions. Thus, when bad weather prolonged the Middle Passage, food and water allowances were reduced. In September of 1781, the slave ship *Zong* sailed from West Africa with a cargo of 470 slaves bound for Jamaica. Twelve weeks later, as it neared its destination, it ran short of water and food. There was also an outbreak of disease on the ship. When the captain saw impending disaster, he proposed jettisoning those slaves who in his view were too sick to recover, reasoning that the insurance underwriters, rather than the owners, would bear the loss. Furthermore, he argued that the action would save slaves from lingering deaths. One hundred and thirty-six slaves were dragged to the deck and flung overboard. Later the underwriters refused to carry the loss.

The constant threat of disease at sea caused captains to maintain some measure of cleanliness and employ doctors. Slave cargoes were afflicted by fevers, dysentery and smallpox, with smallpox having particularly disastrous effects, since there was no cure for it. To those health dangers may be added the torments of seasickness and the oppressive heat in the holds.

Given the oppressive conditions and the yearning for freedom, slaves inevitably revolted against their ordeal. The fear of slave mutinies led to strict controls and stubborn captives were severely punished. Although all would have welcomed the opportunity to escape, slaves from certain areas earned a reputation for rebellion. The so-called 'Coromantees' of the Gold Coast were particularly known for their pride and mutinous behaviour. Often, slaves sought to kill the European traders and set the vessel ashore. Slavers went to great lengths to prevent rebellions and mutinies, visiting the holds daily and searching every corner between the decks for pieces of iron, wood or knives gathered by the slaves. Great care was taken not to leave lying about any object that could be used as a weapon.

Rebellions, contagious diseases, and lack of adequate food compounded the discomfort and difficulty of the passage, which took many African lives. An estimated 3 to 5 per cent of the slaves died before embarkation and another 18 per cent died during the Middle Passage. But this high mortality rate was reduced to about 6 per cent towards the end of the eighteenth century through efforts to achieve better living conditions on ships. Mortality often depended upon the length of the journey to the Americas and the incubating period of diseases, in addition to the conditions aboard ship.

The mortality rate among the crew of the slavers was high. Although death among the slavers did not exceed that of slaves, there was a correlation, which suggests that they were similarly affected by conditions of disease, faulty provisions and length of voyage.

Fig.4
Africans being forced to 'dance' on board ship, from *France Maritime* by Grehan Amedée, Paris, 1855
"While they are upon deck it is thought necessary that they should take exercise; for which purpose the chief mate and boatswain are stationed with a cat of nine tails, to compel them to dance, as it is called." (William James, third mate on *Britannia*, 1768)

'Guineamen': Some Technical Aspects of Slave Ships

M. K. STAMMERS

Guineamen or slave ships were always typical sailing cargo ships of their time up until the abolition of the trade. After that, extreme designs which made speed of sailing to avoid capture the priority over cargo capacity were introduced. These came in a wide range of sizes. They had to sail reasonably well to shorten the Middle Passage as much as possible, and at the same time they had to have sufficient cargo capacity for trade goods and plantation products. They also needed sufficient stability to carry armaments to defend themselves.

Voyages by European mariners were limited by the size, construction and rig of their vessels until the fifteenth century. From about 1450, existing designs such as the 'cog' and the 'hulc' were overtaken by a new type – the full-rigged ship. The 'ship' was at the root of all later developments until the invention of iron-hulled, steam-powered vessels in the nineteenth century. Without it, the slave trade would not have been possible. This new ship design was superior in seaworthiness, sailing ability, size, economy and range of operation to any of its predecessors. Its predecessors were 'shell-built', with their outer skin of planks joined together at their edges. This 'shell' was then made rigid by the insertion of strengthening frames. The new ship was built the other way round. A skeleton consisting of a backbone or keel with stem, sternposts and frames was erected and this was covered with a skin of planks. This change enabled bigger, stronger ships to be built that could carry guns and sufficient men and supplies for long voyages. The implications for long-distance exploration and commercial exploitation are obvious.

It seems likely that this skeleton building technique was first started on the Atlantic coasts of Spain. Allied with it was the introduction of the three-masted sailing rig. In its basic form, this carried square sails on the bowsprit projecting ahead of the ship and on the fore and main masts, and a triangular fore-and-aft lateen sail on the mizzen mast at the stern. The combination of square and fore-and-aft sails made the vessel far more manoeuvrable than its more simply rigged predecessors. Again, like the hull, it was capable of elaboration and development. The first full-rigged ships were carracks. Columbus's *Santa Maria*, which opened up the Atlantic for European exploitation, was probably of this build.

The other important feature of the new ship was that because it was simply built of natural materials, it was self-sustaining. There was virtually nothing aboard that carpenters, blacksmiths or sailmakers in the crew could not renew or repair. Given a sheltered beach, the ship's hull could be careened – cleaned of marine growth, re-caulked and repaired. Spare baulks of timber lashed on deck could be fashioned into replacement masts and spars after storm damage, and bolts of spare canvas could be cut and sewn into new sails.

Within a century of its appearance, the European skeleton-built ship had been sailed right round the world and become the essential vehicle for the opening up of the Americas. That of course included the transport of slaves from Africa. The carrack design was gradually superseded in the sixteenth century. The high bow and stern superstructures made the carrack a formidable floating fortress but at the cost of seaworthiness. The galleon design was narrower and longer in the hull. The high bow structure was removed and the reduction in weight helped to lift the bow, so ensuring the passage of the vessel through the seas. Another feature was an extended platform or beakhead below the bowsprit – a feature continued on eighteenth-century ships in a shortened form.

88
Armed Brig in the Mersey
About 1810, by John Jenkinson (active 1790–1821), oil on canvas, signed

The invention of the 'fluyt' by Dutch shipbuilders about 1600 was the next important development. It was designed as a commercial bulk carrier without the possibility of conversion to an armed vessel. It was flat bottomed, had a higher length to breadth ratio (4:1 up to 6:1), lower superstructure, modest sail plan (to save on crew) and was of lighter construction. It was one of the reasons why the Dutch were able to dominate European sea-trade in the seventeenth century. Many fluyts passed into English ownership as prizes in the mid-century naval wars, and many of their features were incorporated into their English-built successors. However, the fluyt was a slow carrier of low-cost bulk cargoes such as coal, grain or timber, and, although they were used by the Dutch for slaving, they were not particularly successful. In fact, the Dutch used a wide variety of vessels: *hekboot* ('hog boat'), *katschip* ('cat'), *pinas* ('pinnace'), *fregat* ('frigate') and

bark ('barque') in the late seventeenth century. In 1675, the 'jagt' was reckoned to measure 60 feet (18.3 m) in length, the *fregat* 75 feet (22.9 m) and the bark 110 feet (33.6 m).[1]

The 'jagt' was a single-masted vessel with a fore-and-aft rig. Fore-and-aft sails such as triangular staysails (or jibs) were carried on the fore-and-aft standing rigging that supported the masts. Its gaff mainsail was a large quadrilateral sail which was stretched between two spars, a gaff at the top and a boom at the bottom; both pivoted on the aft side of the mast. The combination of gaff mainsail and staysails at the bow made for a highly manoeuvrable, weatherly vessel pointing up into wind as much as 45° as against 60° for a square-rigged vessel. But the majority of slaving vessels were square-rigged.

In the seventeenth century, fore-and-aft sails were added to square-rigged types such as the ship and bark

84
Grand Turk
Exhibition model by W.G. Leavitt, of Salem, Massachusetts

(both three masts) and the 'snow' and 'brig' (both two masts) with resulting improvements in their ability to sail closer to the wind. On long ocean voyages where the wind patterns were relatively constant (for example the Trade Winds in the Atlantic), the square sails came into their own. During the eighteenth century, as the vessels became larger their number increased; so from a main or lower square sail and a topsail in the sixteenth century, masts increased in height for topgallant and royal sails. Light-weather sails known as studding sails which were extended out on spars from the normal sails were introduced in the sixteenth century. These are well illustrated in the sail plan of the *Hall* of 1785. The older method of reducing the size of the main sails by 'bonnets', which were additional pieces of canvas laced to the bottom

of the sail, was phased out by 1750 in favour of 'reef points'. These were short lengths of rope sewn into the sails by which the area of the sail could be reduced to stop the vessel labouring in an increasing wind.

Although there were quite a number of small vessels (as small as 20 tons) in the long-distance trades, the size of the typical vessels slowly increased in the seventeenth and eighteenth centuries. It is impossible to make a comparison across the main slaving nations because of the differences of tonnage measurement. Even for the English merchant marine alone it is difficult because of the changes in the measuring which in any case was fairly inexact before the Registry Act of 1786.[2] As no more than an indication of the changes, the average size of Liverpool vessels according to Stewart-Brown[3] changed thus:

1709	70 tons burthern
1751	under 90 tons burthern
1765	100 tons burthern
1785	under 140 tons burthern
1795	under 160 tons burthern
1800	under 200 tons burthern

This included small coastal traders; but the situation varied from port to port. London, which dominated English shipping in 1700, had large bulk vessels in the east coast trade as well as the very large ships of 400 to 500 tons working for the East India Company. On the whole, there is an impression that the slave ships tended to be larger than average, and towards the end of the era there is a distinction between a West Indiaman which was trading directly and tended to be London-built and a Guineaman engaged in the slave trade which was largely Liverpool- or Bristol-built or owned. However, there were exceptions to this; for example in the case of Lancaster slave ships there was a specialization in smaller brig or snow-rigged vessels.[4] Gomer Williams has a table on the number and tonnage of Liverpool slave ships clearing the port between 1709 and 1807. Unfortunately, he did not give his sources and they must be treated cautiously. They seem to indicate that Liverpool Guineamen after 1730 were always larger than the average ship of the port:[5]

1709	30 tons	1730	74 tons
1751	104 tons	1765	113 tons
1785	139 tons	1797	226 tons
1800	281 tons		

Other European slaving ports seem to have owned vessels of similar size to the Liverpool ones. French ships at Nantes, Bordeaux, etc, were between 200 to 400 tonnes, and the Dutch and Danish vessels lay in a similar range.[6]

The hull shape of a vessel put into the slave trade had to combine a fair turn of speed for the Middle Passage and to avoid attack by enemy warships or privateers with a need to carry a large return cargo from the West Indies. Plans and half-models have survived from 1770 which provide a more detailed view. The half-model of the *Alexander* in the Science Museum's collection at London has fine lines with a sharp bow, raised floors amidships and a good run aft. She is pierced for eighteen guns and has large hatches which suggest she may have been a Guineaman. The lines plan of the French *Joly* in the Guibert Collection at the Mariners' Museum, Newport

News, are even finer.[7] On the other hand, the plan of *Exeter* built at Bristol in 1776 by the Hilhouse family shows a much bluffer hull.[8] The plan of the *Hall* built in Liverpool in 1785 as a West Indiaman which was occasionally dispatched to West Africa was reproduced in 1794 by William Hutchinson in his *Treatise on Naval Architecture*. Hutchinson was the dockmaster at Liverpool who had been a successful privateer commander in his time. His work was one of a growing number of publications on naval architecture. The illustration of the *Hall* includes a sheer elevation, sail and lines plan and, taken in conjunction with the famous plan of the Liverpool ship *Brooks* of 1781, drawn for Parliament in 1786, gives a fairly complete picture of a Liverpool Guineaman of the last quarter of the eighteenth century when that port dominated the business. Their respective dimensions from Liverpool Customs Register were:[9]

	Brooks	*Hall*
length	99.8ft (30.4m)	103ft (31.4 m)
breadth	26.7ft (8.1 m)	29.5ft (9 m)
depth of hold	5.6ft (1.7 m)	5ft (1.5 m)
tonnage	320	375

The tween-deck height where the enslaved Africans were consigned was 5'8" in the *Brooks* and 5'7" in the *Hall*. The *Brooks* plan also shows a platform in the tween deck which projected six feet out from the sides of the ship. She was described as 'frigate built' which meant she was built with a raised afterdeck.[10] The *Hall* was similar and one suspects that this was a necessary feature of any Guineaman because it gave the master and crew a raised position of defence against revolt, which was reinforced with swivel guns and a barricade while at anchor off the West African coast. The *Hall* mounted 22 guns which appears to have been a typical armament – nine-pounders were the most popular size but many had two or four larger-calibre pieces. It seems certain that both ships were designed with slaving as one possible trade; the press notice of the launch of the *Parr* at Liverpool on 18th November 1797, of 566 tons the largest Guineaman, remarked: 'she is looked upon by judges to be a very beautiful vessel and the largest out of this port in the African trade for which she is designed'.[11]

On the other hand, an advertisement for the sale of the French prize *La Vénus* in Gore's *General Advertiser* of 8th January 1801 described her as 'French-built, sails astonishingly fast' and suitable for either a 'voyage for rice or a compleat Guineaman'. She measured 107 feet 'aloft'

86
Ship bowl, 'Success To The Dobson 1770'
Tin-glazed earthenware, Liverpool, 1770

The round voyage could take at least a year. Sacrificial wood sheathing had been used from the late seventeenth century along with a mixture of tallow and sulphur. In about 1779, the Royal Navy introduced an improvement by which all the iron bolts in a ship's hull below the waterline were replaced by copper ones. This made it possible to cover the lower hull with thin copper plates without causing electrolytic action between the iron and copper. The method was so effective that it was rapidly adopted by merchant ships sailing to the tropics. The shortage of suitable ship timber caused the gradual introduction of iron knees (brackets) and hold pillars from about 1790 onwards. Iron anchor cables, which were not only stronger but took much more wear than the traditional hemp cables, were available from about 1800 although rare in merchant ships.

There were also attempts to improve the conditions for the Africans on board. This was partly through limitation of numbers by legislation but also through attempts to improve the ventilation of the slave decks. William Jackson's painting of a Liverpool Guineaman of about 1780–1790 shows a line of port below the gun deck; and the painting of the Danish ship *Fredensberg* of 1787 in the Kronberg Museum shows three large canvas windsails used to force air down the hatches to the Africans below. Boats were also essential to carry cargo and personnel to and from the shore because apart from the home ports like Liverpool, most trading was carried out on anchor. They had to be capable of being rowed and sailed, and in calm weather they were used to tow the ship. The largest could be over 30 feet (9.1 m) long and were rigged as two-masted schooners. They had broad shallow hulls for easy beaching and for stability when carrying. One built by Daniel Brocklebank in 1806 was designed to carry up to 21 hogsheads of sugar.[12]

(on the main deck), with hold and two decks, 22 guns and a tonnage of 480 tons. Even in the decade immediately before the British abolition, Guineamen could be either purpose-built or conversions.

The last quarter of the eighteenth century witnessed other improvements, of which the most important was the introduction of copper sheathing. Tropical marine boring molluscs, especially the teredo worm, were a major source of damage, especially because a ship might have to spend months at anchor delivering and collecting its freight.

85
Watt
Contemporary builders' model, 1797

Notes

1. J. M. Postma, *The Dutch in the Atlantic Slave Trade 1600–1815*, Cambridge 1990, pp. 142–48.

2. D. R. MacGregor, *Fast Sailing Ships, their design and construction, 1775–1875*, 2nd edition, London 1988, pp. 23–25.

3. R. Stewart-Brown, *Liverpool Ships in the 18th century*, Liverpool and London 1932, p. 19.

4. M. Elder, *The Slave Trade and the Economic Development of 18th century Lancaster*, Halifax 1991, pp. 40–41.

5. G. Williams, *History of the Liverpool Privateers and Letters of Marque with an account of the Liverpool slave trade*, London and Liverpool 1897; repr. Liverpool, 2005, p. 628.

6. J. Boudriot, in *Les Anneaux de la Mémoire*, Nantes 1992, pp. 18–19; Postma, *op. cit.*, pp. 142–48; P. Petersen, *Danskernes Slaver*, Kronberg 1983, p. 19.

7. MacGregor, *op. cit.*, p. 35.

8. Hilhouse Collection, National Maritime Museum.

9. These are Customs House Register dimensions and tonnages; the description of the *Brooks* quoted by Gomer Williams, *op. cit.*, p. 585, and the dimensions of Hutchinson's plan of the *Hall* are slightly different. Liverpool Customs Registers, Merseyside Maritime Museum.

10. W. Falconer, *An Universal Dictionary of the Marine*, London, 1780, p. 134: 'implies the disposition of the decks of such merchant ships as have a descent of four or five steps from the quarter deck and forecastle into the waist ...'.

11. Quoted in Stewart-Brown, *op. cit.*, p. 129.

12. Brocklebank Collection, Merseyside Maritime Museum.

87
A Liverpool Slave Ship
About 1780, by William Jackson, (active about 1780–1803), oil on canvas, signed

African Resistance to Enslavement

STEPHEN SMALL AND JAMES WALVIN

Though the slave trade was horrible and morally repugnant, it did not break the spirit, initiative or resilience of the Africans that suffered the rape of their societies and human resources. Africans resisted their bondage from the moment of enslavement; in fact the history of slavery can be written in terms of slave resistance. Africans have always refused to submit to enslavement and have utilized diverse tactics for asserting their humanity and affirming their dignity. Resistance to European domination began from the very point at which Europeans in Africa tried to enslave Africans; and it continued at all times that slavery prevailed.

Any appreciation of African resistance to enslavement must consider the wide range of types of resistance employed by Africans, and people of African origin, to the economic, physical and psychological subordination and humiliation that was part and parcel of enslavement. Resistance to enslavement was collective and it was individual; it was spontaneous and it was planned; it was physical and violent, and it was passive; it was ideological and it was psychological. Resistance was carried out by men, by women and by children; and it took place at local, national and international levels. We need to look at slaves as well as at black people legally defined as free. We also need to consider the less sensational types of resistance on a day-to-day level, as well as some of the more sensational rebellions and insurrections. An understanding of resistance reflects Africans' remarkable resilience against the odds, and helps us to understand the institutions and ideologies developed by black people after slavery was formally abolished.

Africa and the Middle Passage

As enslaved Africans were passed down, in Africa, from their captors to the white traders on the coast, many tried to run away. They tried to escape from the coastal baracoons and slave factories where they were kept before sale to the Europeans. Africans saw their greatest opportunity for escape when being passed across the geography and terrain which was their own. But it was also at this time that the Europeans were at their most vigilant.

The most elaborate precautions against slave runaways and revolt were to be found in the slave castles on the African coast. The castle at Cape Coast in 1682 was 'cut out of the rocky ground, arched and divided into several rooms' underground in such a way that it easily imprisoned a thousand Africans.

Attempts at escape did not cease when Africans had been shackled into the holds of ships. The slave ships were permanently on guard against rebellious slaves, most of whom were ever ready to capitalize on the negligence of their captors. Consequently, revolts on slave ships were commonplace. The greatest danger came at meal and exercise times when Africans exploited their greater freedom of movement.

The slave ship's guns were often trained on its own decks; a reminder that the greatest danger was posed by its own human cargo. The slave captains could never rest easy. On a crossing in 1750, John Newton, a Liverpool slave captain, noted in his journal that he had 'made a timely discovery today that the slaves were forming a plot for insurrection. Surprised two of them attempting to get off their leg irons ...'. On this occasion, a young slave tried to pass a spike through the deck gratings to other slaves. Twenty of them managed to break their chains, but Newton's crew were able to prevent the revolt.[1]

Death of Capt. Ferrer, the Captain of the Amistad, July, 1839.

Don Jose Ruiz and Don Pedro Montez, of the Island of Cuba, having purchased fifty-three slaves at Havana, recently imported from Africa, put them on board the Amistad, Capt. Ferrer, in order to transport them to Principe, another port on the Island of Cuba. After being out from Havana about four days, the African captives on board, in order to obtain their freedom, and return to Africa, armed themselves with cane knives, and rose upon the Captain and crew of the vessel. Capt. Ferrer and the cook of the vessel were killed; two of the crew escaped; Ruiz and Montez were made prisoners.

Fig.5
'Death of Capt. Ferrer, the Captain of the *Amistad*', July 1839, from J.W. Barber, *A History of the Amistad Captives*, 1840
The *Amistad* was taking slaves between ports in Cuba when it was seized by captives who tried to return to Africa

Fig.6
Joseph Cinquez addressing his compatriots on board the Spanish schooner, *Amistad*, 26 Aug 1839.
The crew of the *Amistad* steered the ship to the North American coast. Although captured and tried,
Cinquez and his followers were acquitted because they had been illegally enslaved.

Africans often organized an attack on their kidnappers to seize control of the ship. Sometimes they even succeeded in taking over the entire ship. A well-known example of a successful revolt aboard ship was that of the *Amistad*. In 1839 over 50 slaves, led by Joseph Cinque, took control of a Spanish slave ship, the *Amistad*, and tried to sail it to Africa. They were captured by an American ship before being transported to a United States court and freed to return to Africa.

When they could not seize control of the ship, Africans sometimes jumped overboard, preferring to die rather than to continue in chains.

Slave societies

As soon as they were landed in the colonies, Africans resisted in a wide variety of different ways. The most pervasive and persistent form of resistance was small-scale, individual and not always dramatic, including working slowly, sabotage and running away. Slaves 'went slow' (that is, they were 'artful' in the planters' words; 'playing fool to ketch wise' as the Jamaican proverb maintains), feigning sickness and infirmity; they worked at their own pace, or pretended not to understand instructions – all to the fury of their owners. Slaves frequently spat, urinated in and polluted the masters' food; they also, in moments of desperation, struck back, responding to blows with blows, to curses with curses. Women in particular frequently handed out verbal abuse to whites. Slaves sometimes tried to hurt their owners without getting caught, poisoning their food, harming their children, their property, their animals.

A persistent feature of resistance was running away. The vast majority ran away for short periods, to see family members, friends or loved ones; others escaped for long periods, sometimes years, even decades. Some slaves were never recaptured. Slaves close to the sea or rivers were likely to escape by water; others fled by foot, cart or any other vehicle available. Whatever the practical difficulties, slaves ran away as long as slavery existed, and local newspapers carried regular advertisements for runaway slaves. But running away was not without its consequences: if caught slaves were severely beaten, disfigured or mutilated. The fate of unsuccessful runaways stood as a terrible reminder of what might happen to them.

There were other tragic and heart-rending extremities of resistance – suicide and infanticide – as Africans killed themselves or their loved ones rather than live as slaves. A poignant story is told of Margaret Garner who, having escaped to Ohio from Kentucky in 1856 and been tracked down, killed her daughter (almost decapitating her in an attempt to cut her throat) rather than see her enslaved again. "I will go singing to the gallows rather than be returned to slavery", she insisted.[2]

Another form of resistance was large-scale, collective and dramatic. Revolt was the most spectacular form of slave resistance; it was also – obviously – the most dangerous. It rarely succeeded. More often it incurred the violent fury of slave owners and the colonial authorities. The risks slaves were prepared to take, and the punishments they were prepared to endure, is a statement of how far freedom was cherished.

The number of slave revolts is hard to calculate because it depends on the definition. For example, in the United States, calculations range from nine to 250. Revolts were frequent in the British colonies: in Jamaica, the First Maroon War of 1730–40; in Antigua 1735–36; Stono's Rebellion in South Carolina in 1739; Tackey's Revolt in Jamaica in 1760, which cost about 60 white lives and saw the death of 400 slave rebels, another 100 executed and 500 more transported; Jamaica's Second Maroon War of 1795–96; and Fedor's Rebellion in Grenada in 1795–97.

Curiously, some of the most serious revolts occurred after the slave trade had been abolished in 1807. Bussa's Rebellion in Barbados in 1816 was followed by a revolt in Demerara (Guyana) in 1823 and finally, on the eve of slave emancipation, the Baptist War in Jamaica in 1831–32, the most devastating of all. At its height it involved some 20,000 slaves. The fourteen white deaths provoked a violent reprisal which cost 500 slave lives. The most successful slave revolution was that of Toussaint L'Ouverture in St Domingue in 1791, which led to the establishment of the independent black republic of Haiti.

For most of the history of British slavery, slave revolts were primarily uprisings of Africans and it was only towards the end of slavery (in 1838) that local-born slaves began to play a more leading role. This is understandable in many ways; it was, after all, the Africans who had experienced a life elsewhere and who had endured (and survived) the Atlantic crossing. In the United States 'most leaders were young, literate, married, charismatic men', says Blassingame.[3]

All slave societies had their slave conspiracies, though many of those conspiracies were often the imagination of the whites, ever fearful of their slaves. Any unexplained

178
25 centimes, obverse: palm tree and trophy of arms and flags,
reverse: '25c' in snake 'REPUBLIQUE D'HAYTI AN 13'
Silver, Haiti, Petion Republic, 1816

illness, accident or misunderstood gesture or word was construed as a conspiracy and threat. Wherever conspiracy was imagined or seen, white reprisals were swift and terrible. Whenever revolt actually flared, the planters suppressed it with massive and bloody reprisals and a gruesome tit-for-tat. Slaves knew that if they revolted, they and many others would pay with their lives, normally after excruciating violence. Tackey's Revolt in Antigua in 1735–36 led to at least 86 slaves' executions – 77 of them burned alive. In Barbados in 1816 some 400 slaves were executed; in Demerara in 1823 (in a revolt which involved perhaps 12,000 slaves) some 250 slaves were executed.

From first to last slaves revolted; from first to last they were repressed with an even greater violence. But the fear of death, violence and torture was not enough to quell the spirit for freedom and this dismal litany of violence continued as long as slavery survived in the colonies. And in time, that violence contributed to the planters' undoing. By the early nineteenth century, such levels of reprisals were completely out of kilter with contemporary British feelings. Many in Britain felt that if slavery could only be kept in place by such massive (and counter-productive) acts of violence, perhaps the time had come to end slavery itself.

Maroon communities

One of the most impressive successes of running away was the maroon communities. Maroon communities were free settlements of ex-slaves who lived independently and often waged war on neighbouring planters and other white settlers. These communities were found from very early times in some of the large islands and less settled colonies. As time passed, maroon communities were to be found across the entire spread of the Americas. The whites found it difficult to dislodge and defeat the maroons.

The largest and longest lasting maroon settlements were in areas where whites were small in number and the geography was mountainous, such as South and Central America and the Caribbean. In South America massive communities, some numbering tens of thousands, were to be found from as early as the sixteenth century. But recent evidence from the United States has demonstrated that maroon communities were evident throughout the swamps and mountains of the South, where several communities continued for years raiding plantations, attacking and murdering whites.

Cultural resistance

Resistance was achieved, in the cultural realm, specifically in the areas of religion, music and folk-tales, humour and writing. Africans resisted by sustaining their own collectively created worlds and building for themselves a world far removed from the horrors of their daily lives. These different cultural forms share many aspects in common: as social pastimes and human creativity, as a means to communicate information, ideas, insights, openly or furtively, as commentary and critique on life, and as a vision of the future. In this way, cultural practices supplied the fortitude to confront the harsh realities, and were also a means to retaliate against slave masters in ways not immediately obvious, and thus insulate the slave from retaliation.

The consolidation and transformation of African religions, shaped and sometimes overwhelmed by Christianity, were a source of inspiration. Africans embraced and maintained African religious practices, despite the punishments; both slaves and free blacks established churches, forging spiritual and psychological links with one another. Religion and religious leaders were not just a means of spiritual escape; they were often the mediums through which individuals or groups organized themselves for physical escape. Churches could and did sow the seeds of discord among slaves, particularly those with all black congregations. Collectively religion provided a framework for black organization and self-expression and served as a training ground for black leaders.

Folk-tales across the Americas were clearly influenced by the West African culture in which folk-tales were one of the most important forms. Animal stories pervaded West Africa, including the Nigerian tortoise, the Ghanaian spider

97
Necklace of nine charm pendants
Cloth, leather and horn,
Mande, Gambia

93
Grape shot in bag
Lead, 18th century

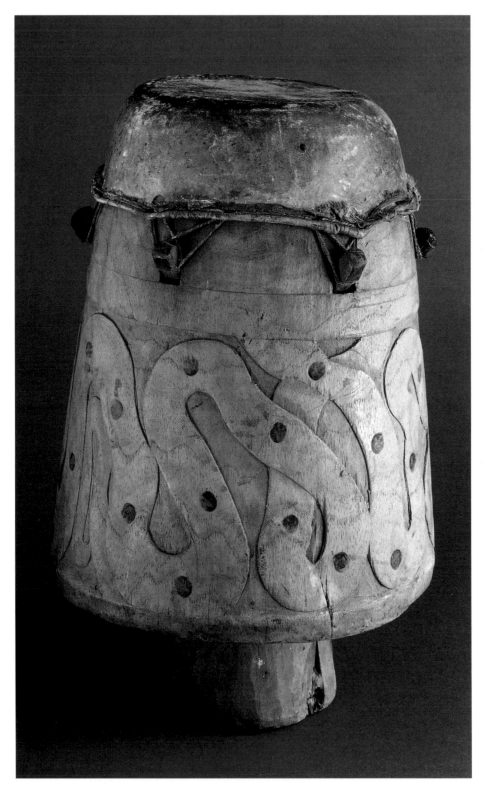

133
Drum, 'The Nanda'
Paramacca tribe, Seeton Ponta Village, Marawyne River, French Guyana

96
Log book of the *Unity*, describing a revolt by slaves on board
1769–71

(or Ananse) and the rabbit. Such creatures were invariably looked down upon by stronger animals, but they invariably outwitted them by being wise, patient and cunning. Parallels with daily life were not lost.

Music and humour fulfilled many of the same functions, communicating ideas and criticizing the slave system and the Europeans that upheld it, and acting as a means of escape from the harshness and depression often caused by slavery. They also enabled the enslaved Africans to attack the system under which they were forced to serve. In humour, there are numerous examples in which blacks made the master look stupid or ignorant, but in a way that only his acceptance or acknowledgement of this would enable him to respond.

The many efforts to read and write, and to use a pen as a means of communication, uplift and encouragement, also characterized slave resistance, from the humble efforts of slaves to learn the basics of reading and writing to the establishment of schools, newspapers and journals by free blacks. Such efforts, widespread though illegal and severely punished by whites during slavery, carried on relentlessly.

Free blacks

There were many black people in slave societies who were not legally slaves. The so-called 'free blacks' were legally free from slavery, but were often subject to identical laws and restrictions of their rights. Particularly in the United States, free black people in the nineteenth century organized and mobilized to end slavery and to secure full equality. This resistance took many forms; some fought for the abolition of slavery, others simply for their own rights. In the United States, for example, by the 1840s, free blacks such as Henry Bibb, William Wells Brown, Frederick Douglass, Lunsford Lane, Sojourner Truth, Harriet Tubman and Samuel R. Ward spoke to anti-slavery audiences throughout the north.

165
Figure of an enslaved African breaking free of his chains
Carved wood, American, late 19th century

A first priority was to avoid being forced back into slavery. Many free African Americans, particularly women, pooled their resources in mutual aid and benevolent associations to protect themselves against destitution. For example, in Philadelphia in 1838, two thirds of the free black benevolent societies were exclusively female, including the Sisterly Union and the Daughters of Absalom. Each member would pay dues and if they fell ill or died they would be given aid or receive a decent burial and their children would be cared for.

A second priority was to abolish slavery. Though the abolitionists' movement was headed mainly by whites, who got most attention, its power and energy came from blacks. Both those who escaped from slavery and those born free supported the work and newspapers of the white abolitionists. For example, William Lloyd Garrison's *Liberator*, founded in 1831, was kept alive by black subscriptions which amounted to 90 per cent of all subscriptions in the first year. David Ruggles, a central figure in the 'Underground Railroad', helped keep up the paper's circulation.

Writing and publication were central to the activities of free black people. One of the most radical written demands for an end to slavery was published early in the nineteenth century. *Walker's Appeal, in Four Articles* by David Walker was most notable for its advocacy of armed rebellion against whites if they refused emancipation. There were others. For example, in 1827, the first black newspaper, *Freedom's Journal*, was started in New York, edited by Samuel Cornish and John Russwurm. The paper lasted only a few years, but many others followed it.

Free blacks were also prominent in the Underground Railroad and they played a major role in aiding runaways. Most 'conductors' (who led the runaways) were themselves escaped slaves, who returned to aid others. Harriet Tubman is reported to have personally helped 300 runaway slaves.

Free black people were active not only within their own nations, but also in establishing international links. Africans throughout the Diaspora travelled to oppose slavery and the oppression and exploitation of Africans. From the United States, activists and educators such as Martin Delany, Edward Wilmott Blydon, Sarah Remond Parker and Alexander Crummel travelled to England and across Europe. In eighteenth-century Britain the work of Olaudah Equiano, Ignatius Sancho and Ottobah Cuguano challenged slavery and the vilification of African societies.

Women's additional struggles

One of the major limitations of existing analyses of resistance is that they have largely ignored the role that women played in actively resisting as well as laying the foundations that enabled men to resist. For example, Bush maintains that 'because the woman was subjected to the same conditions as the male slave, she reacted to enslavement, punishment and coercion in similar ways, from everyday resistance to outright rebellion'.[4] Nor was it just the exploitation and domination of whites that black women had to endure. Bush argues persuasively that 'the slave woman, subjected to both black and white patriarchy, in addition to experiencing class exploitation was also a victim of racism. It is in this framework of triple oppression that her achievements should be measured.'[5]

African women were most likely to resist by talking back to slave masters and overseers. They were also more likely to poison slave owners or contaminate their food. Many invoked mystic curses that were believed to be potent. As cooks and house servants, they were in a privileged position for poisoning and other acts of sabotage.

Free black women were active in a number of ways. Free African American women – including Harriet Tubman, Ellen Craft and Anna Murray Douglass – helped individual slaves gain their freedom, as well as working on the vigilance committees that provided runaway slaves with clothing, food, money and help in finding employment. The Colored Female Religious and Moral Society of Salem, Massachusetts, was formed in 1818, and the Female Anti-Slavery Society of Salem was formed in 1832 by African American women 'to promote the welfare of our colour'. African American women in the abolition movement had to contend with the racism of many white abolitionist women who refused to allow black women to become members of their organizations.

Conclusion

Resistance to slavery is testimony to the indomitable will of the human spirit. As the numerous examples above demonstrate, Africans resisted in a multitude of ways, and for many different purposes. Some resisted every attempt to control their lives; others resisted day-to-day domination; others fought against certain excesses.

Though many Africans were murdered, and many others were psychologically smothered by white domination, the collective will of Africans refused to accept white domination. An understanding of resistance

142
Punishment Records, Friendship Plantation
Jamaica, January–June 1828

demonstrates the variety and vitality of the African spirit. European enslavement of Africans certainly victimized them; but it did not leave them with a victim mentality. Africans were not victims, but survivors.[6]

Notes

1. B. Martin and M. Spurrell (eds.), *The Journal of a Slave Trader – John Newton*, London 1962.
2. Angela Davis, *Women, Race and Class*, The Women's Press, 1981, p. 21.
3. John Blassingame, *The Slave Community*, Oxford University Press, 1972, p. 221.
4. Barbara Bush, *Slave Women in Caribbean Society, 1650–1838*, Heinemann Publishers, 1990, p. 6.
5. *Ibid.*, p. 8.
6. See also Theresa L. Amitt and Julie A. Mattei, *Race, Gender and Work*, Boston, South End Press, 1991; Barbara Christian, 'The Race for Theory', *Feminist Studies*, vol. 14, Spring 1988, pp. 67–79; Paul Gilroy, *The Black Atlantic, Modernity and Double Consciousness*, London and New York, Verso, 1993; Leon Litwack, *Been in the Storm so Long*, Vintage Books, 1977; Orlando Patterson, *The Sociology of Slavery*, Granada Publishing, 1967.

104
Map of St Domingue, printed chart
Jacques Nicolas Bellin, Paris, 1764

105
Map of Jamaica divided into parishes, printed chart
John Ogilby, London, 1671

Caribbean Slave Society

ALISSANDRA CUMMINS

Within the context of West Indian history, slave society is almost synonymous with plantation society. The plantation system gave shape and structure to the ordering of relationships within the islands and put a special stamp on the history of the region. Firmly established during the seventeenth century, it lasted without significant alteration throughout the eighteenth century and continued in a modified form even after slaves were freed in the nineteenth century.

The plantation system was initially established as an economic enterprise geared towards deriving maximum benefits for the planters who owned and controlled it. The plantation and its correlative, slave labour, became the very essence of organized society in the Caribbean. The plantation maintained the balance of power and control within the existing political and social structures and preserved the economic imbalance among the various interest groups.

The plantation system defined an ideology of racism which developed and grew throughout the period of slavery. Its devastating effect is still entrenched in Caribbean society today – three hundred years of human existence translated into economic and political power for the planters, social and economic degradation for the slaves. Rigid stratification ensured the denigration of African cultural systems and the continuing degeneration of the African condition. The myth of white superiority and black dependence was nurtured by forced compliance to the dominant group.

The social structure was caste-like and was firmly supported by legal, political and social developments. There were basically three castes, the whites, the blacks and the coloureds. Due to the volume of the slave trade, the sugar planters were soon heavily outnumbered by their slaves. The black population surpassed the white one in Barbados around 1660, in Jamaica soon after 1670 and in the Leeward Islands soon after 1680. By 1713 there were four blacks to every white in the English colonies. However, the whites maintained their social, economic and political ascendancy through progressive subjugation by legal, military, cultural, material and economic means.

The peculiar nature of Caribbean slavery forces us 'to make a clear distinction between slavery as an abstract legal status and as an actual institution involving economic functions and interpersonal relationships'.[1] This definition of slavery created harsh realities for slaves.

Origins of Caribbean slaves

The sugar planters of Barbados, Jamaica and the Leeward Islands were the first Englishmen to practise slavery on a large scale. Before the close of the seventeenth century they had brought a quarter of a million Africans to the six Islands.

English slaving records from the late seventeenth century are useful in identifying the origins of Africans forced to migrate to the Caribbean. More than 70 per cent of the slaves imported by the Royal African Company from 1673 to 1689 came from the Guinea coasts, with the rest divided equally between the Senegambia region further north and Angola further south. Thus slaves in the Caribbean originated primarily from the Windward Coast (modern Liberia), the Gold Coast (Ghana), and the Slave Coast (Togoland, Dahomey and Western Nigeria).[2]

The English believed that the variety of languages and the intense tribal rivalries among the Guinea Coast peoples hindered enslaved blacks from 'combining' against their

116
One Penny Token, obverse: image of a head 'I SERVE',
reverse: image of a pineapple, 'BARBADOES PENNY 1788'
Copper, Barbados, 1788

masters. A writer of 1694 recorded that the 'safety of the Plantation depends upon having Negroes from all parts of Guiny, who not understanding each other languages and customs, do not, and cannot agree to rebel, as they would do ... when there are too many Negroes from one country'.[3]

English planters were profoundly ignorant and contemptuous of West African cultures. They were satisfied to perpetuate prejudicial stereotypes: the view that Papaws from the Slave Coast were docile and agreeable; that Coromantees from the Gold Coast were proud, brave and rebellious; that Ibos from the Niger Delta were timorous and despondent. All of these were preferable to the Bantu-speaking Angolans who were reputed to be rebellious, bellicose and lazy into the bargain. Time and again the planters underestimated the tenacity of cultural ties. By the end of the eighteenth century most Caribbean slaves were creoles and only a small percentage were African-born.

Daily life

For the vast majority of slaves, life was a long and monotonous routine involving heavy work in the field from 6.00 am to 6.00 pm. The principles and structure of work organization on a plantation created a distinct hierarchical structure not just between white and black but between the house slaves, the field slaves and the artisans. It was a system based not on merit but on age, proximity and sex, with the work gangs at the bottom of the structure and the household workers nearest their masters at the top.

Blacks were dependent for most of their necessities of food, clothing and shelter. On the plantation slaves were generally housed in a row of little oblong huts, built out of sticks and cane trash, facing on to a yard. Each hut was modestly furnished with a sleeping mat, a cooking pot and one or two calabash gourds cut to make cups or spoons. In town very few negroes were permitted inside their masters' houses but lived segregated in small huts behind.[4]

Health was also often related to status, and the rigours of field labour clearly had a negative effect on the longevity of these workers. The list of illnesses which pervaded the eighteenth- and nineteenth-century slave population included consumption, dysentery, dropsy, yaws, yellow fever, elephantiasis and tetanus. But most critical of all was malnutrition.[5] While some slave laws specified the basic food necessities, compliance was by no means universal. Dunn records that the slaves ate a monotonous, meagre and starchy diet of cassava, corn, plantain, beans and yams, supplemented by rum on Saturdays, and meat whenever an animal died of disease. In fact there is some evidence that planters underfed slaves in order to help break their resistance.

Slave laws – control of slaves

During the seventeenth century, sugar planters created one of the harshest systems of servitude in Western history, the repercussions of which continue to be felt as we move into the twenty-first century. Lacking English precedents to draw upon, the colonists quickly adopted the system brought to the West Indies by the Spanish and worked up a legal code and a set of customs that divided island society starkly into two classes, white masters and black slaves.[6] The Negro was defined as a chattel and treated as a piece of conveyable property, without rights or redress in law. This differed starkly from older forms of bondage in classical antiquity because of its racist character. Slavery in the English islands was ruthlessly exploitative from the outset and nakedly racial – a device to maximize sugar production and as cheaply as possible.

Supposedly, the English did not at first distinguish in any meaningful way between white indentured servants and the Negroes who arrived from Africa. White and black labourers were equally unfree, the only real difference being that whites served for specified terms, and blacks served indefinitely. But this is surely not a valid interpretation given the immediate categorization of Africans as heathen brutes to be treated as chattels.[7]

While it is true that the English colonists initially avoided defining the nature of slavery, they worked out the problem pragmatically and built up piecemeal a regulatory structure governing their relations with slaves. In 1637 in Barbados the Government Council decreed that 'Negroes and Indians, that came here to be sold, should serve for life,

125
Auction hammer
Ivory with silver band, (?) 19th century

unless a contract was before made to the contrary'. While this might apply to some of the Indians, no contracts seem to have been made with any Negroes.

The problem of interracial sex soon arose. In 1644 the Antigua assembly composed a law against miscegenation, forbidding 'caarnall coppullation between Christian and Heathen', the latter defined as Negroes and Indians. A freeman or free woman who fornicated with a black was fined. A servant had his or her term of indenture extended. The offending heathen was branded or shipped. A mulatto child produced by a mixed union was enslaved until age eighteen or twenty-one (and in 1672 this was extended to life).[8]

Since the planters did not want to assimilate or acculturate such an alien population, they segregated themselves socially and culturally from the blacks to preserve their own identity. Thus to maintain control a system was devised to intimidate, police and discipline the slaves. The slave laws enacted by the island legislatures in the seventeenth century, therefore, tell us a good deal about the treatment of Negroes and the character of slavery in the Caribbean colonies.

By 1661 Barbados had a comprehensive slave code. The Act passed by the Barbados assembly 'for the better ordering and governing of Negroes' was the most important piece of legislation issued in the island in the seventeenth century. The preamble to this document assumes that Negro slaves are chattels for it undertakes 'to protect them as wee doe men's other goods and chattles'. It was re-enacted with slight modification by later Barbados assemblies in 1676, 1682 and 1688 and was copied by the Assemblies in Jamaica (1664), South Carolina (1696) and Antigua (1702).

In 1685 another law tried to shut down the Sunday markets by prohibiting white persons from trading with Negroes for pots of sugar and jars of molasses filled from their masters' pots. The slave laws legitimized a state of war between blacks and whites, sanctified rigid segregation and institutionalized an early warning system against slave revolts.

The slave code accorded masters, servants and slaves carefully differentiated rights and obligations, with the master being given almost total authority over his slaves and much less power over his servants. Slaves' lives could be forfeited for relatively minor crimes and their bodies mutilated for even more minor transgressions. While slave conspiracies and uprisings abound as evidence of the

Fig.7
'Cutting sugar cane' from H. T. de la Beche, *Notes on Jamaica*, 1825
Sugar cultivation was very labour-intensive. Harvesting involved long hours
of arduous, back-breaking work, by men, women and children.

Fig.8
Insurrection on board a slave ship from W. Fox, *Brief History*, 1851
Uprisings on board ship happened regularly and were put down with brutal ferocity.

188
Plate with scene of former slave family in front of cabin, 'FREEDOM FIRST OF AUGUST 1838'
White earthenware with blue transfer-printing

113
24 Shilling Piece, silver
Danish West Indies, 1767

blacks' unequal struggle, little is known of their attempts to control their reality, through their day-to-day social and economic activities. By the eighteenth century, an elaborate and comprehensive superstructure had been established which confirmed indubitably the ideology of slaves as property. It is a rather exquisite irony that much of the emphasis of law-making from this period went into protecting the planters' property from themselves.

African-Caribbean culture

Caribbean culture is difficult to interpret in terms of its origins, and questions of identity and tradition continue to plague Caribbean people. The persistence of African cultural continuities in African-American and Caribbean societies has also been used to serve different, and opposite, ideological ends.

The violent uprooting of Africans from their homeland to enslavement certainly took its toll on the integrity of African culture in the Caribbean. Although the Africans brought a set of systems – socio-hierarchical kinship, beliefs, languages – to the Caribbean many of them were almost destroyed by slavery. The uneven distribution of power and lack of contact with home cultures meant that Africans had to undergo drastic cultural accommodation – acculturation.[9]

Slaves brought to the Caribbean from the West sub-Saharan African region (Senegal to Angola) emerged from an area of great ethnic diversity. Nevertheless there is an underlying unity in a number of shared cultural features.

Despite the large number of African languages used within the West and Central regions there was a linguistic unity within the area and slaves in the Caribbean who came from different ethnic groups were able to communicate with each other. While there was great diversity in the words of the various languages and dialects used, there was a general similarity in the grammar used. Caribbean languages have retained a number of African words in modern use. However, the main African influences lie in the language systems. Also the sentence structure, pitch tone, the combination of sound (e.g. suck teeth) and gesture (e.g. cut-eye), an open syllable structure, all have their origins in African language systems. A major feature of linguistic transfer from Africa to the Caribbean is the proverb, highlighting a pervasive African world view and philosophy, as well as a simple way of putting things that is typical of that area.[10]

Finally in the Caribbean there evolved several common creole patois, comprising European and African elements,

103
Plan of Havana, with inset map of Cuba
John Hinton, from the Universal Magazine, London c.1762

Fig.9
Map of Barbados, by John Ogilvy, London, mid-17th century
This map includes drawings of a sugar press and crops such as sugar cane, pawpaw and pineapple.

Fig.10
'Cutting sugar cane' from W. Clark, *Ten Views in Antigua*, 1823

Fig.11
'Shipping the sugar' from W. Clark, *Ten Views of Antigua*, 1823
Antigua was one of the main sugar-producing islands of the Brtitish West Indies.

which ensured communication among the slaves. As a general rule Caribbean languages are not seen as belonging to the African tradition but are judged against Greco-Roman norms of language structure: for example, inflections are regarded as the essential part of the ideal language structure. Creole languages tend, therefore, to be negatively evaluated in relation to these norms. Those which have managed to escape this stigma have progressed (or are progressing) to the status of official and national languages (e.g. Papiamentu) and are positive symbols of national identity.

African religious beliefs were also assimilated into the culture. The Asante-derived religion of the maroons of Surinam and Jamaica recognized Dahomean and Bantu deities and the Dahomean religion of Haiti contains Yoruba deities. The tradition of religious syncretism (fusion of African and Christian religions) is typical in the creole religious forms of Shango, Vaudun, Punkumina and Santeria. In Jamaica, for example, the Asante-based religion of the maroons and Kumina, based on the Bantu religion, have given way to Pukumina with its observance of both Christian and African deities. After this came Revivalism, which preserved ancestor veneration and spirit possession. Certain Caribbean religious forms such as spirit possession have been assigned an African frame of reference.[11]

Indigenous economic systems in the Caribbean were much influenced by the West African traditions of credits and marketing. Thus traditional Southern Nigerian rotating credit and savings associations, termed the *esusu* (Yoruba) or the *isusu* (Igbo), were also established in the islands where they were known as 'the hand' and 'pardners', or regionally as 'susu'. They still remain in use today. Higgling and peddling formed the backbone of the islands' internal marketing system, based on West African forms of bartering produce for goods. These systems, which were adapted by enslaved Africans throughout the Diaspora, have now developed into an intricate regional network.

Games, too, have played an important socializing role in the community. Found all over Africa, the popular game 'mankala' or 'warri' (*owari*) in West Africa made its way to the Caribbean and became part of the African cultural legacy of the region. The game is a challenge to dexterity, calculation, anticipation and artistry. Traditionally played only by men (or in a few cases by women of superior status) 'warri' was played in public and involves great audience participation. For the Bush Negroes in Surinam, warri was

not simply a game but maintained many of the customary patterns and social etiquettes associated with it in Africa. In Barbados and Trinidad, for example, the game was often played as part of a wake for the dead.

Caribbean folk-tales, Anansi stories or stories featuring a spider and other animals existed in the pre-slavery culture of slaves. They expressed a morality which the Africans brought with them and, more importantly, they form part of the African narrative and performance traditions which were important parts of African communal interaction that helped mould new African-Caribbean communities.

Notes

1. D. B. Davis, *The Problems of Slavery in Western Cultures*, New York 1966, p. 25.
2. For a more detailed analysis of the volume of the slave trade see P. D. Curtin, *The Atlantic Slave Trade: A Census*, Madison 1969, pp. 122–23, 128–30.
3. An excellent reference work on slave origins is R. S. Dunn, *Sugar and Slaves: The rise of the planter class in the West Indies, 1624–1713*, London 1973, esp. pp. 229–38. See also K. G. Davies, *The Royal African Company*, pp. 213–33.
4. Early slave life has been described in detail in R. Ligon, *A True and Exact History of the Island of Barbados*, London 1657. Hans Sloane, *A Voyage to the Islands of Madera, Barbados, Nieves, S. Christophers and Jamaica*, London 1707–25, is similarly useful, if somewhat ethnocentric in its observations.
5. K. F. Kiple, *The Caribbean Slave: A Biological History*, Cambridge 1984, pp. 76–103, offers fascinating insights into the effects of disease and sickness on the survival of enslaved Africans.
6. E. V. Goveia, *Slave Society in the British Leeward Islands*, Yale, 1965, pp. 152–202, still remains the acknowledged authority on this topic.
7. Dunn, *op. cit.*, p. 227.
8. Leeward Islands MSS Laws, 1644–1673, C.O. 154/1/49–51.
9. Aspects of the African Caribbean cultural experience have been analysed in depth in G. K. Lewis, *The Growth of the Modern West Indies*, New York and London 1968, pp. 30–54.
10. Valuable sources on the development of Caribbean languages include M. Alleyne, *Root of Jamaican Culture*, London, Pluto Press, 1988.
11. R. F. Thompson, *Flash of the Spirit: African and Afro-American Art and Philosophy*, New York 1983, pp. 16–31, 163–179, offers a valuable insight into the origins of existing forms of religious syncretism in the Caribbean.

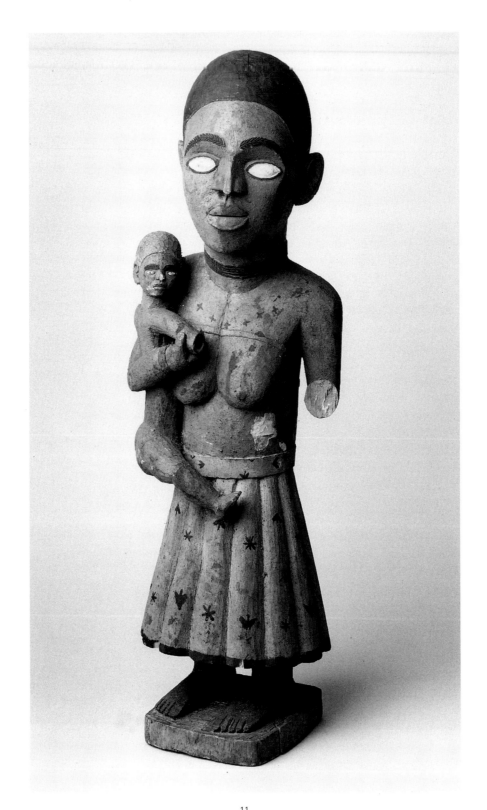

11
Carving of a woman and child
Carved and painted wood, Lualli River, Cacongo, West Central Africa, 19th century

Women in Slavery and the Transatlantic Slave Trade

JENNIFER LYLE MORGAN

The transatlantic slave trade was a human atrocity that has yet to be duplicated. The millions of men and women transported from sub-Saharan Africa, as well as those left behind, experienced a degree of dislocation, grief and cultural devastation that is difficult for contemporary researchers, readers or museum-goers to comprehend.

Our understanding of the trade and its consequences is still being refined. Like many historical events, many of our images of the trade are incomplete or, indeed, misleading. Erroneous impressions of enslaved Africans – snatched by strangers, bereft of spirit or culture, incapable of resisting their enslavement – have become part of our inherited vision. These impressions bar a more complex and accurate understanding of the slave trade and its significance for those men and women who were enslaved.

Understanding the particular experience of enslaved women in the slave trade is especially important. As a minority of the total number of the enslaved, women's experience in slavery and the slave trade has largely been disregarded. At best, historians have assumed that the generic term 'slave' encompassed both men and women. However, the particular experiences of African women and their female descendants had particular consequences upon the experience of enslavement – both for themselves and for their male counterparts. Women's access to particular components of their African society's culture, their agricultural work, and their sexual and reproductive identities are just three of the elements that we must look towards in order to assess the impact of the transatlantic slave trade fully.

Many European observers of West and West Central Africa commented upon the industry of African women. They saw them as constant workers, some even characterizing these women as drudges or 'slaves'. While these observations are coloured by the Eurocentric perspective of the observers, they are, nonetheless, important windows into the lives of African women and men prior to and during the disruption caused by the transatlantic slave trade. Jean Barbot, one of the more frequent European travellers to Africa, was quite struck by the place of women in the societies he encountered. He noted that women were the primary agricultural workers, as well as the household member responsible for cooking and child-rearing. Barbot was often confused by African behaviour, particularly when it did not correspond to 'proper' male and female conduct. He found it difficult to understand the role that men played in society, and fell back upon the simplistic formulation that they did nothing, and were examples of the 'laziness' of 'Africans'. When approached by traders on one of his voyages, Barbot saw the group of men and women approaching his ship as 'traders and their wives' – clearly it was outside his realm of possibility that the women were traders in their own right. As the primary producers of some manufactured goods – thread and cloth, for example – it is conceivable that women would have, rightly, been at the forefront of trading and economic exchanges with the newly arriving Europeans. This despite English visitors' inability to understand social behaviour unfamiliar to them.[1]

European traders were similarly troubled by the freedom with which African women approached them. Many Europeans ascribed licentiousness and sexual immorality to African women. The independence that characterized some African women's lives, as well as their relative state of undress in comparison with the women with which European men were familiar, led to

19
Calabash
With inscribed geometrical patterns, Rabba, Nigeria, 1860

20
Calabash
Painted with geometrical designs in red and black, Garoua, Cameroon

12
Carving of a woman in a cloth skirt
Carved and painted wood, with (?) printed cotton skirt, Winneba, Ghana, 19th century

RUNAWAY from the subscriber, a likely mulatto girl, named Betsey-Ann. Whoever will apprehend and lodge her in the Cage, or deliver her to the subscriber, or to Mr. Jacob West in St. Thomas's parish, shall receive Six Dollars reward, and whoever will give information of her being harboured by any white or free person, shall be entitled to one half of whatever can be recovered by law. She is supposed to be harboured at Mr. Samuel Hackett's in Black Rock, or at Thorp's estate. Masters of vessels are forbid taking her off the island, and if she returns home of her own accord, she shall be pardoned.
ANN HACKETT.

RUNAWAY from the subscribers, a tall thin, black skin woman, named Abigail, has lost one of her fore teeth and is a little hard of hearing, she is well known in town and country, being accustomed to carry about goods for sale. Whoever will deliver the said woman at the estate of John Lane, esq; called Black Rock, or lodge her in the Cage, giving information thereof, shall receive six dollars, and any person who will give information of her being harboured by any white or free coloured person, shall be further rewarded with Five Pounds on full conviction of such offender.
ELIZABETH BURKE.
☞ All Masters of vessels are desired to be cautious of the above woman.

Fig.12
Advertisement for runaways, from *Barbados Mercury*,
Saturday 7 January 1797
Slaves regularly ran away from their owners, many to the maroon communities which existed in all parts of the Americas.

WHEREAS a Negro Woman Slave, named ROSE, well known in this Island, the Property of Mr. *David Kidd*, who has for some Time past absconded from his Service, did this Day in Mr. *Kidd's* Absence from the Island, in a felonious manner enter into his House and take therefrom sundry Articles. This is to give Notice, That if any Person or Persons shall apprehend the said Negro Woman ROSE, and deliver her to the Subscriber in *Kingstown*, he or they shall be handsomely rewarded.----And all Persons are requested not to harbour her, as they will answer it at their Peril.
JOSEPH FRASER.
Kingstown, Oct. 3, 1789.

Fig.13
Advertisement for a runaway female slave, from *The Royal St Vincent Gazette and General Advertiser*, Saturday 10 October 1789
Women generally ran away for short periods and feature less frequently in runaway advertisements.

assumptions that African men and women lived in a loose and ungoverned state. Sexuality, and its corollary chastity, acted as symbols of civilization as far as European observers were concerned. As they assessed African women's sexuality, they drew conclusions about African humanity that would have very important consequences – most important being the widespread acceptance that African people deserved mass enslavement at the hands of European colonists.

As previously mentioned, African men and women were not enslaved in equal numbers. The majority of those enslaved by all European nations throughout the period of the transatlantic slave trade were men. One might assume that women were not as highly valued as labourers by Europeans who believed that women were weaker and poorer workers; that the basis for the imbalance was located in European attitudes and assumptions. However, those women who were enslaved in the Americas were never 'protected' by European owners from hard labour; they were exploited in the sugar, rice and cotton fields. The explanation why women were not enslaved by Europeans in the same numbers as their male counterparts is found in Africa. The central position that African women occupied in their own societies as agricultural and craft producers meant that, from the onset, there were fewer women available to European purchasers. But there were very few women who were not forced to labour somewhere; many women were enslaved on the African continent or sold into the Occidental slave trade. Most slaves in Africa were, in fact, women; a testament to women's importance as labourers. Those Africans sold on the transatlantic slave trade were the men and women who were not highly valued, for whatever reason, by the men and women who made them available to European purchasers.[2]

The gendered nature of the transatlantic slave trade had very important consequences for those women and men who were not enslaved by Europeans. In African societies up and down the west coast of the continent, social relations and interactions were invariably altered as more and more men were taken from their shores. Over the course of the seventeenth and eighteenth centuries women became the significant majority of some African societies, outnumbering men by as much as two to one. At the same time, the number of women enslaved in Africa increased. Nonetheless, in a crucial departure from women's experience in the Americas, many slave women in African societies were integrated into slave-owning families as

143
Receipt from Court of Baltimore to Mr R O'Ferrale for payment of $1000 for female slaves
Baltimore, 5 September 1859

'junior co-wives'. The children born of these marriages were evidence of women's social mobility. One can only speculate how men and women's lives in African societies were altered on a day-to-day basis as a result of these shifts in gender ratios. But one must assume that the reverberations encompassed almost all aspects of society – work, culture and family life.[3]

It is true that those men and women who remained on the African continent suffered consequences of the transatlantic slave trade, but certainly their sufferings paled in comparison to those who were transported from their ancestral home to a new life of strange lands, strange peoples and forced labour. Even before their arrival in the Americas, enslaved Africans endured the Middle Passage – a period in which one's sense of future was wrenched away as one bore an interminable wait.

Once African men and women arrived at the coast, they were confined in fortresses and castles until the arrival of ships from Europe that would take them to the Americas. So-called 'castle working slaves' were obtained for the fortresses. The Royal African Company stipulated that these be half women and half men. At these fortresses women were subjected to the sexual demands of the white men who were stationed there to oversee the business of enslavement. These factors, as they were called, required enslaved women to clean and cook for them, as well as to submit to sexual advances. The only thing that could work in the favour of these women was that they were subjected to a stable situation which could ultimately provide them with means to escape or manoeuvre. Other women and men, however, were not held at fortresses but were sold in small numbers to ships that would make their way slowly along a river coastline. This method could mean, for those among the first to be enslaved, weeks on board a ship before setting out on open sea. In this situation as well, women were particularly vulnerable to exploitation and

Fig.14
'A Female Negro Slave, with a Weight chained to her Ankle',
from J. G. Stedman, *Narrative of a five year expedition against the
Revolted Negroes of Surinam*, 1772–77, London, 1796
Means of restraint were frequently cumbersome and cruel.

assault on the part of European sailors anxious to give vent to their sexual appetites.[4]

Once a loaded slave ship left the African coast, the seven- to eight-week journey to the Americas began. On many ships, women were allowed a limited degree of freedom that was denied to enslaved men. While men were confined to the hold of the ship at almost all times, women were often allowed to remain above decks, sometimes without the shackles which bound the men day and night. The women's relative freedom of mobility allowed them to move about and communicate with one another in a fashion which men could not. In some cases, as on board the *Amistad* in 1839, women took advantage of that freedom to plan revolts or attacks upon the white sailors who enslaved them. For most women, however, time above deck meant unwanted exposure. It subjected them to rape and attack from sailors. Some women were impregnated by

sailors during the journey. Others, whose misfortune it was to give birth on board, saw their infants thrown into the sea since they were too young to bring a good price at the auction block. For many women, the Middle Passage – a time of unspeakable horror and degradation for all enslaved Africans – was a period of sexual brutalization that could have only served as a bleak foreshadowing of what was to come.[5]

Once a slave ship arrived at its destination the enslaved women and men were 'cleaned up' and put on display for potential buyers. Slave purchasers often complained that ships arrived with their 'human cargoes' badly diseased and damaged. Much of that sickness was the result of inadequate food and water during the Middle Passage, as well as the diseases which were the inevitable result of the human excrement that was allowed to build up in the holds of the slave ships. Potential purchasers of these women and men therefore felt it their right to examine their 'property' intimately, subjecting the enslaved to an excruciating violation of their bodies. At this moment, one would imagine, the sexual violation that had been the sole fate of many women, both prior to and during the journey, became somewhat universal.

After being purchased and surviving the 'seasoning' period, during which those enslaved women and men who did not die had time to adapt to their new environment, the newly enslaved would be put to work. Although life in the Americas for the enslaved is primarily understood through this lens of work, other important components affected the communities in which enslaved men and women lived. One of those components was simply the inability to create lives with one another. Until the mid-eighteenth century in North America, slave societies could not reproduce themselves, because of low birth rates, high infant mortality, and the exorbitant toll of disease. Newly enslaved Africans had continually to be added to existing populations in order to maintain their numbers. In the period directly preceding the American War of Independence, for the first time the influx of new Africans was no longer necessary in the Southern colonies; babies were born and were surviving to adulthood.[6]

Clearly, one of the most important factors in the ability of a population to reproduce itself is the number of women. In most Caribbean slave societies it was not until the nineteenth century, in some cases not until after slavery had been abolished, that this reproduction was possible. Consequently, the entire cultural life of a slave society was

141
Letter to Thomas Eaton, Swansea, from his slave, Pheba
Kingston, Jamaica, 12 March 1793

linked to the presence or absence of women. In those areas, like the West Indies, where women were relatively absent and where there was a constant stream of newly enslaved African arrivals, religious and cultural links to African societies remained tangibly evident well into the nineteenth and twentieth centuries. In areas like the Southern North American colonies, however, where women's presence was more significant, African cultural forms became less decisive as a distinctly African-American, or creole, culture developed. This creolization of culture was also accompanied by a particular agony. In the colonies of Maryland, Virginia, North Carolina, South Carolina and Georgia, there developed in the late eighteenth and early nineteenth century an internal slave trade that had terrible consequences for the enslaved. These states began to supply the states of the lower South – Alabama, Mississippi, Louisiana, Florida, Texas – with slaves born in the upper South. Parents and children were wrenched apart and families devastated as slave-owners profited from the demand for slaves that they were now able to fill.

Plainly, the nature of slavery in the Americas varied considerably over time and space. This was true in the realm of work as well as in terms of reproduction and its consequences. The lives of enslaved Africans taken to Mexico in the sixteenth century, Jamaica in the seventeenth century, Virginia in the eighteenth century or Cuba in the nineteenth century were extraordinarily different from one another. Enslavement was not a static experience. It made a significant difference whether one was enslaved in a Mexican silver mine, on a Pennsylvanian ship, or on a South Carolina rice plantation.

Nevertheless, in terms of work, slavery for women did sustain a certain static quality. Enslaved women's lives in the Americas were characterized, above all, by incessant work. Slave societies developed around the production of export crops: the West Indies produced sugar and coffee, the Chesapeake produced tobacco, the American South produced cotton and rice. However, it is not the case that all slaves in Virginia, for example, were picking and growing tobacco. As a slave society developed there were roads and bridges to be built, bricks to be made, houses and buildings to be constructed, cattle to be tended, horses to be shod, clothes to be sewn, boats to be loaded and ships to be sailed. Most of these jobs were done by enslaved Africans; none of them was done by women. Those who escaped field work, with the exception of a small number of domestic workers, were all men. So while some men could elude the monotony and hardship of the field, almost all women were required to spend their working lives cutting, gathering and stacking sugar cane, wading ankle deep in rice fields, or bent over cotton bolls.[7]

Ironically, the innovation that made these crops successful in the Americas came from the knowledge and experience brought by women. The agricultural skills which most African women brought with them to the Americas were, whether consciously or not, manipulated by white slave-owners. All the crops, with the exception of sugar, developed in the Americas by planters anxious for profit were ones commonly cultivated on the West African coast. Indigo, tobacco and rice, to name a few, were crops with which African women were far more experienced than European men. Enslaved men brought different skills. White colonists in South Carolina, for example, learned cattle-raising techniques from African men. Women's past role as agricultural workers prepared them for the work of the fields. One can only assume that for enslaved men the indignity of enslavement was intensified by being forced to do what, at home, was categorized as women's work.[8]

The household work – cooking, serving, child-tending – traditionally associated with female slaves was not the lot of most women during most of the period of slavery. The Caribbean, for example, was a place to which planters came without their families, intending to become rich and leave – if they came at all. Many simply hired a man to oversee the running of a plantation in their absence; there were few households that required 'staff'. It was not until the nineteenth century that white planters in many parts of the Americas turned their attention to the social niceties that came with acquired wealth and stability. As white society developed and domestic servants were needed, the chance to leave the field may have been welcomed by some enslaved women. Others, however, may have felt that the proximity to whites that came with domestic duties was distasteful or dangerous or both. Many enslaved domestic servants found themselves on duty for twenty-four hours a day, sleeping on the floor outside the doors of their owners, and only rarely seeing their own family. Cooks were sometimes fitted with masks to prevent them from eating from the kitchen; those who were not so fitted were supervised by whites convinced that all blacks were thieves and dishonest. The paranoia of slave owners meant that domestic servants were constantly accused of poisoning or plotting to kill their owners. In some instances, those accusations were real. The proximity of domestic slaves to owners meant they were in the prime position to initiate revolt or rebellion. In other cases slave-owners were simply venting their generalized fear by falsely punishing the individual slaves with whom they came in closest contact.

The close contact between owner and slave brought with it some very complex relationships. For example, slave women were routinely employed as wet nurses, or 'Mammies' for the white children who would grow to own them. High infant mortality among the enslaved meant that an enslaved woman would be given no time to grieve over the death of her infant before she was forced to put a white infant to her breast. It is difficult to imagine the tangle of resentment and tenderness felt by a woman in this position.[9]

Similarly complicated was the existence of sexual relationships between enslaved women and slave-owners. Some women were victims of rape, exposed to the unwanted and relentless sexual demands of men who wielded unchecked power over them. On the other hand, some used longer-term sexual relationships with slave-owners as a means towards obtaining better living conditions for themselves and their families, always aware of the fact that the relationship's future was entirely out of their hands. Although real affection between slave and slave-owner could exist, it was often overshadowed by the realities of power. Women who found themselves in the role of 'mammy' or 'mistress' were women whose emotional lives were manipulated by slave-owners. They were expected to nurture those who owned them. They were expected to be loyal, loving and sexually available. They were expected to put the needs of their owner and his or her family before those of their own. When they submitted to the expectations of slave-owners they did so under force. Some women probably came to identify their own needs with those of their owners. Others resisted that identification and maintained an independent sense of identity and community. Neither endured the relationship without acquiring scars – physical or psychological.

There is no question that personal relationships between owners and slaves existed. Evidence for them can be found in the population of enslaved women and men who were freed or 'manumitted'. Despite being significantly

192
Token, obverse: a kneeling woman, 'Am I not a woman and a sister 1838',
reverse: 'United States of America Liberty 1838'
United States of America, 1838

outnumbered by men in the slave community, in the freed population women equalled, if not outnumbered, men. Women were manumitted in greater numbers than men throughout North America. Freed populations in North America were disproportionately female. Enslaved women were freed as a result of their association with slave-owners, or when female children, who were manumitted at a rate higher than male children, were freed with their mothers. This is not to say that the freed populations were born only of sexual relationships. Male and female domestic servants were manumitted for long service and 'loyalty'. In most slave societies, some slaves were manumitted for performing military services – although, clearly, these were always men. Likewise, slaves could purchase their freedom with money made from hiring their services out. An artisan would pay a fee to his owner for the privilege of working outside the plantation; he could then save his remaining wages to purchase himself out of slavery. Nonetheless, like those who served in the military, those who had skills to be hired out were, in all likelihood, male. It was therefore only in those societies in which slaves were allowed to purchase their freedom, or where there were substantial numbers of military conflicts, that the freed population was more equally balanced between male and female.[10]

Manumission was not simply a benevolent impulse. By manumitting a domestic servant or long-time labourer, a slave-owner abrogated his responsibility to care for an aged or disabled slave, male or female, who could no longer work. By allowing some slaves to purchase their freedom, slave-owners provided a controlled outlet, something to strive for, that instilled determined hard work among some of the enslaved. By rewarding military service, slave-owners encouraged the enslaved to identify themselves with those who owned them; uniting slave and slave-owners against a 'common' enemy.

Manumission was not, however, a common experience. Most enslaved women and men lived their entire lives without hope of obtaining their freedom. This did not stop many from attempting to take freedom for themselves. The parameters of enslavement for women – the decreased mobility in contrast to men, the lack of variety in their work, the proximity to slave-owners when doing domestic labour – shaped the form of resistance which most women chose. There were few full-scale slave rebellions in the American South, and among those that did occur women were rarely in the forefront. The revolutionary efforts of the Stono Rebellion in colonial South Carolina, the nineteenth-century struggles of Denmark Vesey in Louisiana or Nat Turner in Virginia were planned and executed by enslaved men whose mobility allowed them to traverse communities spreading information and conferring on strategy. When examining the resistance patterns of enslaved women, one finds women combatting slavery on more individual ground. In their capacity as domestics, women's most extreme form of revolt was the murder, most often through poison, of slaveholders. Less extreme forms of resistance included work slow-downs, the theft of food to feed themselves and their families, and the refusal to perform certain tasks. Resistance also took the form of running away. For women, who often had familial ties that dictated their ability to disappear completely, running away was often cyclical. A woman would disappear for a week or so, after which time she would return having illustrated to the slaveholder her ability to fly in the face of his or her orders. Men, who were less likely to have intimate family ties as a result of their majority presence in slave communities, were more likely to absent themselves on a permanent basis. Slaveholders who were faced with what they saw as a permanent attempt to run away would place advertisements in the local newspapers describing their absent 'property'. In colonial South Carolina, for example, the only women who appear in these advertisements are those who have run away with a man and children or in family groups.[11]

In slave societies in Latin America and the Caribbean, a form of resistance known as 'marronage' was far more common than in the American South. Runaway slaves would come together in geographically isolated regions to form maroon societies – Africans and their descendants who lived, often in battle with white soldiers and slave-owners attempting to destroy them, independently. As it happened, marronage also took place in societies in which women were vastly outnumbered by men. Nevertheless, records of these communities are replete with mention of women and children, suggesting that women were particularly eager to create a space in which it was possibly to live, and raise children, freely.[12]

Ultimately, of course, the battles that enslaved women and men fought to obtain individual or collective freedom were successful. There are a few women whose names are still evident in the historical record: Nanny, the eighteenth-century Jamaican maroon leader, Sojourner Truth, the former slave who obtained her freedom and spoke widely on the evils of slavery during the struggle for abolition, and Harriet Tubman, who made over 300 trips from the American South to the North, leading countless slaves to freedom. These women, however, are exceptional; most enslaved women and men remain nameless. As these individuals struggled to create stable lives and communities in the aftermath of enslavement, their experiences continued to be shaped by the particulars of gender. There are those who have argued that, in the Caribbean, women actually experienced a reduction in mobility and economic independence as formerly enslaved women and men embraced the European conventions of male and female behaviour during slavery's aftermath. Regardless of the truth of that claim, it is true that one of the defining symbols of freedom was the ability for African-American and Caribbean women to work in their own homes, providing the care and sustenance for their families that was denied them during enslavement. As it is during enslavement, so in the aftermath of slavery the particular experience of women is a central key to understanding slavery's impact upon the African-American and Caribbean communities.[13]

Notes

1. See John Barbot, *A Description of the Coasts of North and South Guinea ... in A. Churchill (ed.), A Collection of Voyages ...*, London, 1732; and Claire Robertson and Martin Klein (eds.), *Women and Slavery in Africa*, Wisconsin, University of Wisconsin Press, 1983.

2. See Herbert Klein, 'African Women in the Atlantic Slave Trade', in Robertson and Klein, *Women and Slavery in Africa*, pp. 29–38.

3. See John Thornton, 'Sexual Demography: The Impact of the Slave Trade on Family Structure', in *Women and Slavery in Africa*, pp. 39–48; Susan Herlin Broadhead, 'Slave Wives, Free Sisters: Bakongo Women and Slavery c.1700–1850', in *Women and Slavery in Africa*, pp. 160–184; and Robin Law, *The Slave Coast of West Africa, 1550–1750; The Impact of the Atlantic Slave Trade on an African Society*, Oxford, Oxford University Press, 1981; Joseph Miller, *Way of Death: Merchant Capitalism and the Angolan Slave Trade, 1730–1830*, Madison, University of Wisconsin Press, 1988.

4. See Records of the Royal African Company, T70 series, Public Record Office, London.

5. See Howard Jones, *Mutiny on the Amistad; the Saga of a Slave Revolt and its Impact on American Abolition, Law, and Diplomacy*, New York and London, Oxford University Press, 1987; Colin Palmer, *Human Cargoes: The British Slave Trade to Spanish America, 1700–1739*, Urbana, University of Illinois Press, 1981; James Rawley, *The Transatlantic Slave Trade: A History*, New York, W. W. Norton & Company, 1981.

6. See Allan Kulikoff, *Tobacco and Slaves; The Development of Southern Cultures in the Chesapeake, 1680–1800*, especially 'Black Society', pp. 317–436, Chapel Hill, University of North Carolina Press, 1986.

7. See Jacqueline Jones, *Labor of Love, Labor of Sorrow; Black Women, Work, and the Family, from Slavery to the Present*, New York, Basic Books, 1985.

8. See Daniel Littlefield, *Rice and Slaves: Ethnicity and the Slave Trade in Colonial South Carolina*, Chapter 4, 'Rice Cultivation and the Slave Trade', pp. 74–114, Baton Rouge and London, Louisiana State University Press, 1981; and Peter H. Wood, *Black Majority: Negroes in Colonial South Carolina from 1670 through the Stono Rebellion*, Chapter 4, 'Black Pioneers', pp. 95–130, New York, Knopf, 1974.

9. See Barbara Bush, *Slave Women in Caribbean Society 1650–1838*, Chapter 2, '"The Eye of the Beholder": Contemporary European Images of Black Women', pp. 11–22, London, James Currey, 1990. Deborah Gray White, *Ar'n't I a Woman? Female Slaves in the Plantation South*, Chapter 1, 'Jezebel and Mammy: The Mythology of Female Slavery', pp. 27–61, New York, W. W. Norton, 1985.

10. See Ira Berlin, *Slaves Without Masters; The Free Negro in the Antebellum South*, especially Part 1, 'The Emergence of the Free Negro Caste, 1775–1812', pp. 15–134, New York, Vintage Books, 1976; and David Cohen and Jack Greene (eds.), *Neither Slave Nor Free: The Freedman of African Descent in the Slave Societies of the New World*, Baltimore, The Johns Hopkins University Press, 1972.

11. See Deborah Gray White, *Ar'n't I a Woman?*, especially Chapter 2, 'The Nature of Female Slavery', pp. 62–90; Barbara Bush, *Slave Women in Caribbean Society*, especially Chapter 5, 'The Woman Slave and Slave Resistance', pp. 51–82; Herbert Aptheker, *American Negro Slave Revolts*, 5th edition, New York, International Publishers, 1987 (first edition, Columbia University Press, 1943); and Eugene D. Genovese, *From Rebellion to Revolution; Afro-American Slave Revolts in the Making of the New World*, New York, Vintage Books, 1981.

12. See Richard Price, *Maroon Societies; Rebel Slave Communities in the Americas*, 2nd edition, Baltimore, The Johns Hopkins University Press, 1979.

13. See Marietta Morrissey, *Slave Women in the New World: Gender Stratification in the Caribbean*, Lawrence, University Press of Kansas, 1989 for the thesis of women's reduced freedoms in the aftermath of slavery. See also Herbert Gutman, *The Black Family in Slavery and Freedom, 1750–1925*, New York, Vintage Press, 1976; Jacqueline Jones, *Labor of Love, Labor of Sorrow*; Leon Litwack, *Been in the Storm so Long: the Aftermath of Slavery*, New York, Vintage Press, 1980.

Liverpool and the English Slave Trade

DAVID RICHARDSON

English involvement in the African slave trade is generally thought to have begun in the mid-sixteenth century when John Hawkins made his celebrated voyages to West Africa and the Caribbean in the 1560s. But only with the 'sugar Revolution' in Barbados in the 1640s and the resulting growth of demand for African labour in English America did the English become regular participants in the trade in African slaves. From 1660 to 1698 England's trade to Africa was dominated by London-based companies chartered by Charles II, the most important being the Royal African Company which held a monopoly of English trade to the continent from 1672 to 1698. The company's charter was challenged by 'interlopers' or private English traders, and was also strongly criticized by sugar planters who claimed that it failed to supply sufficient slaves to meet their needs. However, it is clear that by the end of the seventeenth century, largely as a result of the Royal African Company's activities, the English had become the largest traffickers in slaves in the Western world, shipping on average some 6–8,000 enslaved Africans a year to the Americas, over twice as many as the Dutch, their closest competitors.

The ending of the Royal African Company's monopoly in 1698 allowed private merchants legally to enter the slave trade. Thereafter, shipments of slaves in English vessels rose dramatically, averaging over 20,000 a year throughout most of the first half of the eighteenth century and reaching 30–45,000 a year during the rest of the century. The evidence suggests that, overall, almost 11,000 ships were fitted out in England for the slave trade between 1698 and 1807 and may have been responsible for transporting about three million Africans into slavery. This was equivalent to just under half of the estimated 6.7

million slaves shipped from Africa to America in the eighteenth century.

Merchants at London and Bristol dominated the English slave trade before 1730 and continued to be involved in it throughout the rest of the century. However, Liverpool ships began to enter the slave trade from the beginning of the century – the first known Liverpool slaver being the *Blessing*, which set out for Guinea in August 1700[1] – and by 1730 around fifteen ships a year were leaving the port for the African coast. Thereafter, the number of ships fitted out in Liverpool for the slave trade climbed fairly steadily, growing to fifty or more a year in the 1750s and to just over one hundred a year in the early 1770s. Numbers of clearances from Liverpool to Africa then fell back during the War of American Independence in 1775–83. But they recovered strongly during the years after the war and reached 120–130 a year during the decade immediately preceding the abolition of the British slave trade in 1807.[2]

Of the 11,000 ships dispatched from England to Africa in the eighteenth century, approximately 5,300 (or 48 per cent) departed from Liverpool. Most of the remaining 5,700 slavers left from London and Bristol. These totals tend to underestimate the growing influence of Liverpool over the English slave trade as the eighteenth century progressed. Between 1780 and 1807 over three quarters of all English ships involved in the English slave trade were fitted out in the port. Thus Liverpool was not only the largest single English slaving port in the eighteenth century, but after 1780, it was also the undisputed slaving capital of England and by far the largest slave port in the Atlantic world.

The reasons for Liverpool's rise to dominance of the English slave trade have long been debated. One argument offered is that, relatively marginalized in the transatlantic

Fig.15
The Goree Warehouses, St George's Dock, Liverpool, by Samuel Austin, 1829
Named after the French island fortress off Senegal, the original warehouses were destroyed by fire in 1802 and rebuilt in 1811.

sugar and tobacco trades before 1750, Liverpool merchants proved more enterprising as slave traders than their rivals in London and Bristol. It is claimed, for instance, that they were more prepared than merchants at other ports to supply slaves illegally to the colonies of other nations, notably Spain and France.[3] Other writers have drawn attention to competitive advantages that Liverpool traders derived from the low level of wage rates in Lancashire before 1750, improvements in local port facilities, the relative freedom in wartime of Liverpool ships from attacks by enemy ships in British waters, and access to cotton textiles and other goods in demand in Africa. However, the relative importance of these factors is uncertain, and there still remains much room for debate about the causes of Liverpool's success as a slave port.

It is misleading to picture eighteenth-century Liverpool simply as a slave port. The city's merchants had close trading links with Ireland and western and southern Europe that preceded their involvement in the slave trade, and these continued to develop even as their interest in slaving grew. Furthermore, trade with other parts of the Atlantic world increased after 1700. Although Liverpool was never the principal English importer of sugar or tobacco, trade with the West Indies and the Chesapeake region in North America grew substantially in the eighteenth century. There was also a significant expansion of trade with the Newfoundland and Greenland fisheries and with the colonies of white settlement north of Maryland. For most eighteenth-century Liverpool merchants, therefore, slave-trading was only one of a number of commercial pursuits followed.

Despite this proliferation of trading interests, it is clear that the traffic in enslaved Africans was the cornerstone of Liverpool overseas trade from about 1730 to 1807. This is reflected in the proportion of the port's shipping tonnage that was involved in the African trade. Thus during the

177
Oval épergne, by Pitts and Preedy, engraved with the arms of the Town of Liverpool and those of Machell
of Penny Bridge Co. Lancaster, impaling Penny, with inscription. Presented to James Penny in 1792
by the Liverpool Town Council in recognition of his support for the slave trade.
Silver plate, 1792

152
Punch pot
Hand painted with gilt decoration, earthenware, black ground, 1766

78
Guinea
Gold, Royal African Company, 1663

1730s about one sixth of Liverpool-owned shipping tonnage was involved each year in slaving voyages. This rose to over a quarter between 1750 and 1775. Thereafter, despite further increases in the tonnage of ships sent to Africa, the share of Liverpool shipping committed to slaving declined as trade with other areas, including the Americas, grew even faster. Even in the last years of the Liverpool slave trade, however, the African trade still employed about one sixth of the Liverpool fleet.[4] In addition, it appears that throughout the second half of the eighteenth century Liverpool merchants employed as much tonnage of shipping in trade with the West Indies as they did to Africa. Given the failure of newly imported African slaves to reproduce in the islands, the West Indies depended heavily on regular supplies of new African slaves to sustain their production of sugar and other exports. Moreover, some of the sugar and other goods carried from the islands by 'direct traders' comprised payments for African slaves delivered by other ships. In several ways, therefore, the slave trade was intimately linked with the growth of direct trade between Liverpool and the Caribbean. Taking this into account, it appears that the African and related trades may have occupied at least a third and possibly up to a half of Liverpool shipping tonnage in the half century before 1807.

Most of the ships sent from Liverpool to Africa were owned by Liverpudlians. We can only estimate the amount of capital that Liverpool merchants invested in the slave trade. It is clear that equipping ships for a slaving voyage to Africa was expensive, necessitating expenditures on the ship and its fittings, the hire of a crew of up to 40 or 50 men, the provision of foodstuffs for the slaves in the Middle Passage, and the purchase of a cargo of trade goods to barter for slaves at the African coast. Among the trade goods shipped were Indian fabrics, Manchester cottons, copper and brass wares, beads, liquor, firearms, and gunpowder. From merchants' accounts, it appears that the average cost of putting a slave ship to sea in the mid-eighteenth century was about £4,000, two thirds of which consisted of expenditures on trade goods.[5] As ships increased in size and the price of slaves in Africa rose, the cost of outfitting a slave ship mounted, reaching about £10–12,000 by the end of the century.[6] When combined with estimates of annual clearances to Africa, these figures suggest that about £200,000 a year was invested at Liverpool in the slave trade around 1750. This sum may have risen to over £1,000,000 a year by 1800.

The Liverpool slave trade attracted investment by individuals living in northern Lancashire and Cumbria, the West Riding of Yorkshire and the west Midlands. But most of the capital invested in the trade came from merchants, tradesman and shipmasters living in Liverpool and adjacent towns. To fund and organize voyages, these investors formed partnerships, the membership of which ranged in most cases from about three to eight individuals, though smaller or even larger partnerships can be discovered. Contemporary accounts suggest that the Liverpool slave trade attracted large numbers of small and occasional investors. But most of the funding and organization of the port's slaving activities revolved around a core of substantial and regular investors drawn mainly from the élite of eighteenth-century Liverpool commercial families such as the Blundells, Crosbies, Earles, Heywoods and Tarletons. As the trade in slaves was usually regarded as financially risky, the larger investors in the trade tended to spread their funds across several voyages simultaneously.

The contribution of the slave trade to the prosperity of eighteenth-century Liverpool cannot be measured precisely. Almost certainly, however, it was substantial. Historians continue to debate how profitable the slave trade was. Profits varied widely from voyage to voyage and some voyages were financial disasters, particularly where large numbers of slaves died in the notorious Atlantic crossing from Africa to America. Overall, returns on investments in the trade seem, nevertheless, to have averaged about 8 to 10 per cent a year in the second half of the eighteenth century.[7] Not surprisingly, investment in the African trade helped to bring substantial wealth to some of the principal Liverpool slave traders. For instance, John Tarleton, a major mid-eighteenth-century African and West Indian merchant who became Mayor of the city in 1764,

82
Thomas Golightly, a leading Liverpool merchant and Mayor of the city, who was involved
in the slave trade and listed among 'the Company of Merchants trading to Africa' in 1807.
British School, oil on canvas, 19th century

saw his fortune climb from £6,000 in 1748 to nearly £80,000 in 1773.[8] Similarly, Thomas Leyland, who was a major slave merchant after 1783, co-founder of the bank of Leyland and Bullins, and several times Mayor of Liverpool, was reputed to have been worth over £736,000 just before his death in 1827.[9]

While the slave trade helped to enrich some of the leading merchant families of Liverpool, it also brought employment and economic opportunities for many others in the city and surrounding towns. Some local merchants gained by supplying trade goods on commission to slave ships or by handling the sugar and other slave-produced goods imported in vessels returning from the Americas. Manufacturers in Warrington, St Helens and Manchester prospered through supplying the copper goods, glassware and cotton textiles that were exchanged for slaves at the African coast. Local tradesmen and seamen in Liverpool found work in building, fitting out, and manning the 50 to 100 ships that regularly left Liverpool each year for Africa in the second half of the eighteenth century. Large proportions of those who sailed on slave ships failed, of course, to return to Liverpool, in many cases succumbing, like the Africans they were expected to supervise, to disease and ill treatment in the course of voyages. At the same time, some suppliers of goods and other services to the slave fleet went bankrupt, victims perhaps of the financial uncertainties that surrounded the trade. Overall, however, the trade in enslaved Africans was a vital pillar of the eighteenth-century Liverpool economy, underpinning the substantial increase in the city's trade and shipping and promoting closer connections with the industrializing towns of Lancashire. Given such benefits, it is hardly surprising to find that Liverpool merchants were among the most vocal opponents of British abolition of the slave trade in 1807.

In retrospect, the fears of contemporaries about the impact of abolition upon Liverpool's fortunes proved to be misguided. Although prevented by law after 1807 from participating directly in the shipping of slaves, Liverpool merchants as well as Manchester manufacturers continued to supply English-produced trade goods to Spanish and Portuguese slave traders based in Cuba and Brazil throughout the early nineteenth century. In addition, Liverpool remained a significant importer of West Indian sugar and emerged after 1815 as the principal importer not only in England but in Europe of American raw cotton and West African palm oil. Both the latter were essential to the

'Industrial Revolution' that was occurring in north-west England at this time. Enslaved black labour was fundamental to the growth of both West Indian sugar until 1833 and raw cotton in the Southern United States until 1861. Moreover, it appears that much of the palm oil imported into Liverpool in the century after 1815 was produced by local slave labour within West Africa. Thus the shadow of slavery and the slave trade continued to hang over Liverpool's commercial history long after the city's status as the slaving capital of the Atlantic world had been ended by Parliamentary abolition of the English slave trade in 1807.

Notes

1. Liverpool Record Office, Norris Mss.
2. All figures relating to clearances are from D. Richardson, 'The Eighteenth-Century British Slave Trade: Estimates of its Volume and Coastal Distribution in Africa', *Research in Economic History*, xii, 1989, pp. 185–95.
3. [James Wallace], *A General and Descriptive History of the Ancient and Present State of the Town of Liverpool*, Liverpool 1795.
4. For figures on clearances from Liverpool to Africa and all overseas destinations, see Liverpool Record Office, Holt and Gregson papers, 942 HOL X, 361–65, XIX, 69–71.
5. D. Richardson, 'Profits in the Liverpool Slave Trade: the Accounts of William Davenport, 1757–1784', in R. Anstey and P.E.H. Hair (eds.), *Liverpool, the African Slave Trade, and Abolition*, Liverpool, 1976.
6. R. Anstey, *The Atlantic Slave Trade and Abolition 1760–1810*, London 1975.
7. Richardson, 'Profits in the Liverpool Slave Trade'; Anstey, *Atlantic Slave Trade*.
8. Liverpool Record Office, Tarleton papers, 920 TAR 2/1.
9. L. Pressnell, *Country Banking in the Industrial Revolution*, Oxford 1956, p. 419. Accounts relating to Leyland's slaving voyages are to be found in Liverpool Record Office, Leyland Papers, 387 MD 40–4; Harold Cohen Library, University of Liverpool, Ms. 10/46–52.

Oil not Slaves: Liverpool and West Africa after 1807

ANTHONY TIBBLES

The abolition of the slave trade by the British Parliament in 1807 might have been expected to have had a catastrophic effect on the economy of Liverpool. This was not the case, principally because Liverpool merchants continued to expand their bilateral trade with the Caribbean and the United States in those very goods – sugar, rum and increasingly tobacco and cotton – which had formed one arm of the triangular trade. Needless to say, these commodities were produced on plantations which were to rely on slave labour for many decades to come.

It is also true that Liverpool merchants continued to trade with West Africa, though on a more limited and less notorious basis. Initially attention focused on the goods which had brought Europeans to the West African coast before the large-scale involvement with slaving – gold, ivory and pepper. However, as early as 1800 small quantities of palm oil had been imported into Liverpool and it was this product which was to become the main trading interest for the next 100 years or more.[1]

Palm oil, extracted from the berries of palm trees, was recognized as a good lubricant and an important ingredient in soap. The introduction of metal machinery into industrial processes (for instance in the textile industry) brought with it a need for lubrication not found in smaller hand-operated machines. From the 1830s demand was spurred by the requirements of the railways. In the home, there was a rapidly growing demand for soap, particularly as industrial workers undertook dirtier jobs.

The pioneers of the trade came from Liverpool and were the same merchants who had been active in the slave trade: such men as John Tobin, James Penny, Jonas Bold and the Aspinall brothers. They used their experience and contacts in West Africa to develop this new trade. There was also a familiarity about it. The goods they were exporting were identical to those of the slave trade era, predominantly textiles, rum and guns. The Liverpool merchants quickly established a tight hold on the trade and sought to maintain a monopoly, which they were successful in doing for more than half a century.

The trade saw substantial growth and substantial profit. A case in point is the career of John Tobin, who was Mayor of Liverpool in 1819 and was knighted two years later.[2] He was born in 1763 and had been involved in the slave trade first as a master and then as an owner. After 1807 he continued to trade to West Africa and was an early participant in the palm oil trade. In 1814 he imported 450 tons of oil. By 1832 this had risen to 4,000 tons. One of the main reasons for Tobin's success seems to have been his friendship and alliance with Duke Ephraim, an African chief at Calabar, who by the 1820s had a virtual monopoly of all trade in the area.[3] Others were similarly successful. By 1834 Tobin estimated that the trade in palm oil was worth half a million pounds.[4]

By this time the activities of the surviving slave traders, now dubbed 'illegal trade', were being seen as a frustration to what was referred to as the 'legitimate trade'. It was, therefore, for both economic and moral reasons that efforts were made to stamp out the slave traders and the British, who only a few decades before had been the major participants in the slave trade, became the major opponents. Anti-slavery patrols had been instigated in 1808 and in the 1820s, 1830s and 1840s up to a third of the Royal Navy was deployed off the West African coast. Not unnaturally some Africans found this confusing. Obi Ossai, King of Abo, put the matter very succinctly: 'White people first told us we should sell slaves to them and we sold them; and White people are now telling us not to sell slaves. If White people give up buying, Black people will give up selling.'[5]

54
'An Accurate / MAP of / AFRICA / from the Best / Authorities'
London, 18th century

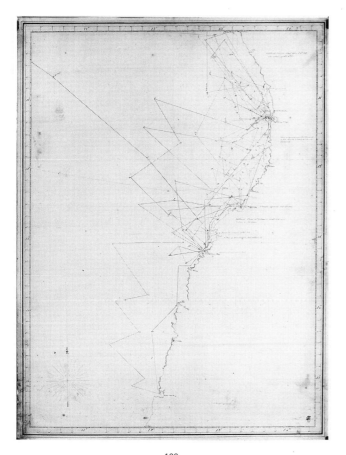

193
Manuscript Chart showing the tracks of a Royal Navy
patrol vessel off the West African Coast
Facsimile of chart by Edward Smith, 1843

By the early 1830s some of the new generation of merchants were becoming frustrated with the problems of the coastal trade and began considering direct trading links inland. They were encouraged by the explorations of the Lander brothers who had established the course of the Niger and shown that it provided a direct route into the interior. They not only recognized the commercial opportunities it offered but also saw it as a means of dealing a blow to the trade in slaves. The argument ran that only by encouraging proper trade, by encouraging Africans to produce raw materials that Europeans wanted to buy, and by introducing Christianity, could the slave trade be eliminated. They were naturally opposed by the coastal traders and by the African middlemen who saw this as a threat to their livelihoods.

Again, the leaders of this movement were based in Liverpool and two of the main exponents were MacGregor Laird and Robert Jamieson. Both were Scottish by origin. Laird was born in Greenock in 1808 and was a son of William

Laird, founder of the shipbuilding firm. His African activities are relatively well known. In particular, he instigated and led an expedition to the Niger in 1832, building two steamships, the *Alburkah* and the *Quorra*, in Liverpool for the purpose. The expedition was a total failure: of 48 men only nine survived (highlighting one of the principal obstacles – the climate and problems of fever and disease). Laird lost a lot of money and, though continuing to support the cause, withdrew from active involvement for almost twenty years.

The standard was taken up by Robert Jamieson. Originally from Glasgow, he settled in Liverpool in the early 1830s (though from 1836 he also maintained a London home). He had extensive trading interests in South America, India and China, but was also involved in the palm oil trade. In 1839 he ordered a paddle steamer, which he named *Ethiope*, from the Liverpool shipbuilder, Thomas Wilson. The vessel left Liverpool in September 1839 and once in West Africa was placed under the command of John Beecroft, a man who had many years' experience as merchant and agent and was later to become British Consul at Fernando Po.

Beecroft's mission was to find a channel into the main body of the Niger, which avoided 'the pestiferous swamps of the Delta' and to 'establish a commercial intercourse with the interior'.[6] He was successful in finding a route through to the main river and in travelling to Rabba some 400 miles from the coast.

However, the voyage also confirmed the difficulties of any inland trading enterprise: 'It remains then that commerce on the Niger can only be followed by means of steam-vessels manned entirely by native Africans, under the direction of European officers and engineers well inured to the climate. But even in this mode of prosecuting the desired intercourse, there appears too formidable an array of difficulties to render it likely to become of any considerable practical benefit to Africa or Europe – first, in the danger of navigating to and from Africa, vessels constructed so as to be of sufficiently light draught of water for the ascent of the rivers, and consequently badly adapted to the open sea – next, in the great expense attendant on the employment of steam-vessels in so distant a quarter and in such a climate – then in the impossibility of having them repaired in case of accident to the engineers, or of any serious injury to the machinery; and finally, in the fact, now well ascertained, that the river itself is not navigable except during the few months of the year when it is flooded.'[7] Despite this frustrating conclusion, Jamieson instructed Beecroft to attempt an alternative route to the interior via the Old Calabar and Cross Rivers further east.

Meanwhile the efforts to establish trade with the interior were receiving support from another quarter, the British government of Lord Melbourne. It backed a so-called Niger Expedition which attempted to establish a European-style farm in the Lower Niger, and three Royal Navy steamers arrived in the river in 1841. In fact, the expedition was opposed by many of those who might have been expected to welcome the initiative, including Jamieson and Laird. Jamieson was strongly against it and wrote three pamphlets on the subject starting with *An Appeal to the Government and People of Great Britain against the Proposed Niger Expedition* which he published in 1840. His case was economic – that free trade was superior to government intervention. He argued that once Europeans were given government money and became involved in agriculture, they would want to protect their interest. They would want a chartered company, then a monopoly. It would force prices down, discourage African farmers who would cease to work towards a market economy and all development would end.

The expedition was a total failure, but for a more immediate and obvious reason, namely fever. The settlers were decimated: 48 of the 145 were dead within two months and Jamieson's own *Ethiope* was called to assist in the rescue, escorting HM *Albert* down the Niger and back to Fernando Po.

Ethiope returned to Liverpool in 1843 but made further explorations of the Niger in 1845 and 1846. These voyages only confirmed Beecroft's initial assessment and although Jamieson continued to trade in palm oil he seems to have effectively given up exploration. However, the desire to establish direct trade inland did not die. In the mid-1850s MacGregor Laird returned to the scene and again undertook a series of expeditions into the interior using a number of new steam vessels which he built for the purpose. It was on one of these expeditions, under Dr Baikie, that the medical problem was eased when the efficacious effects of quinine were established. However, his attempts to set up trading stations were opposed by African middlemen and his ships were attacked on several occasions.

During his last years, Laird was preoccupied with these affairs, though writing in September 1858 he appears rather disillusioned: 'I suppose by next mail I shall hear something decided from the Niger, either that the *Sunbeam* is lost going up the river or has got up, or that she has put back under some pretence or other; if she is lost I am insured, if she has got up, I have no doubt she will make something of her cargo, if she has put back it will be a ruinous business – here again

I have lost all confidence in the judgment of the man in charge of my property, I blame myself severely for going so headlong into such an outlay, as usual I see now what others could clearly see, whose passions and judgments were not warped by constantly thinking and dreaming of one idea, that the Agents you send out have quite a different standard to your own – they go to make money and that alone. I think they would make more by following their instructions but few can see more than immediate results.'[8]

Despite these setbacks Laird and Jamieson continued to believe in the desirability of establishing trade with the interior. In his *Commerce in Africa*, published in 1859, Jamieson urged the use of an alternative land route from the Cross River to the Niger as the way to avoid the swamps of the Delta. It was, however, another of MacGregor Laird's initiatives which had the most profound effect on the way trade was to be conducted between Britain and West Africa in the future. In 1849 Laird founded the African Steamship Company and in 1852 contracted with the British Government to provide regular steamship services to carry the mails between England and West Africa.[9] This effectively gave him a subsidy for the new steam service. The introduction of steam liner services had a major impact on the palm oil trade and Liverpool's role in the region.

During the 1840s and 1850s, Liverpool's monopoly of trade in the region had been challenged by the entry of a number of small-scale merchants from Bristol and London eager to take advantage of the lucrative returns on palm oil. For a while, up to a third of the trade was taken by these new traders and Laird's initial decision to run the new steamer services from London seemed likely to reinforce this trend. However, in 1856 he relocated the steamers to Liverpool. Although the numbers of traders continued to increase, they used the new steam ships rather than their own vessels or tramp sailing ships and gravitated to Liverpool as the centre of their operations.[10] Gradually the monopoly was re-established and by 1880 virtually all British palm oil imports were coming through Liverpool once more.

Ironically, at the West African end the opposite situation took place. Steamers could easily call at more ports and the effect was to diversify the sources of palm oil. The regularity and reliability of the services also drew other cargoes to the steamers so that Liverpool became the centre of virtually all West African trade. The Liverpool-based shipping companies and their owners who ran the services worked closely together and saw off competition from other ports. By establishing agreed charges they protected their own

Fig.16
The Paddle Steamer *Ethiope* off the West Coast of Africa, about 1840,
by Samuel Walters (1811-1882), oil on canvas

positions. In later years this situation was consolidated by Sir Alfred Jones, who ran Elder Dempster, the main company, from 1884. Indeed, until recent years the name Elder Dempster was synonymous with the West African trade.

There was one further consequence of Liverpool's monopoly of the trade with West Africa. As Africans had been brought into Liverpool in the eighteenth century as a result of the slave trade, so these new trading links brought Africans into the port in the two centuries which followed. Elder Dempster employed Africans, particularly Kroomen, for much of the heavy work on board ship, though on poorer wages and conditions than their white counterparts. Many of these seamen found temporary residence in Liverpool and some established themselves permanently. In this way they contributed to the development of the black community in the city.

The links which the slave trade established between Liverpool and West Africa have endured for nearly three centuries. Despite the abolition of the trade in 1807, Liverpool's merchants found ways to exploit the experience which they had built up over the previous decades. Just as they had dominated the old 'African Trade', so they monopolized the new situation. The consequences of Liverpool's relationship with West Africa have been profound and far-reaching.

Notes

1. K. O. Dike, *Trade and Politics in the Niger Delta, 1830–1885*, Oxford 1956.
2. M. Lynn, 'Trade and Politics in 19th Century Liverpool: The Tobin and Horsfall families and Liverpool's African Trade', in *Transactions of the Historic Society for Lancashire and Cheshire*, cxlii, 1993, pp. 99–120.
3. A. J. H. Latham, 'A Trading Alliance: Sir John Tobin and Duke Ephraim' in *History Today, xxiv*, 1974.
4. For a discussion on the profitability of the trade see M. Lynn, 'The Profitability of the Early Nineteenth Century Palm Oil Trade' in *African Economic History*, 1992, pp. 77–97.
5. Dike, *op. cit.*, p. 48.
6. 'On Benin and the Upper Course of the River Quorra or Niger', communicated by Robert Jamieson, *Journal of the Royal Geographical Society*, 1841, pp. 184–193.
7. *Ibid.*
8. NMGM, Archives, DX.
9. P. N. Davies, *The Trade Makers*, London, 1973.
10. M. Lynn, 'From Sail to Steam: The Impact of the Steamship Services on the British Palm Oil Trade with West Africa, 1850–1890', *Journal of African History, xxx*, 1989, pp. 227–45.

Fig.17
'Lowest Life in London', by George Cruickshank, 1823

161
Olaudah Equiano
British School, late 18th century

Black People in Britain

JAMES WALVIN

Black people have lived in Britain for centuries. During the Roman occupation, for instance, a unit of African troops was stationed near Carlisle. There is evidence of Africans in York in the same period. Africans similarly found their way to many parts of Europe in the course of the Middle Ages. But from the late fifteenth century references to blacks begin to increase. There were a number of Africans at the court of King James IV of Scotland about 1500. Dunbar's poem *Ane Blak Moir* celebrated one such at the royal court.

By the last years of Elizabeth I, blacks were to be seen in London. Indeed, in 1596, the Queen sent a letter to the Lord Mayor of London complaining that: 'Her Majesty's understanding ... there are of late divers blackamoores brought into these realms, of which kind there are already here to manie [too many], considering how God had blessed this land with great increase of people'. The question arose again in a royal proclamation in 1601 which declared that the Queen 'is highly disconcerted to understand the great number of Negroes and blackamoores which (as she is informed) are carried into this realm since the troubles between her highness and the King of Spain ... [and] also for that the most of them are infidels having no understanding of Christ or his Gospel: hath given special commandment that the said kind of people shall be with all speed avoided and discharged out of this Her Majesty's realms'.

It seems that a number of these Africans were free people, possibly seized and freed from captured Portuguese and Spanish vessels. However, some Africans were brought directly to England. Early merchant adventurers had been instructed to import Africans and with the development of the early slave trade Africans began to acquire a price and a social cachet. Time and again, British writers spoke of the exotic nature of black people living in Britain. The imported Africans were objects of fascination for people who had rarely seen black humanity before. Indeed, at royal masques and balls it was even common for people to dress up and blacken their faces.

However, once the British began to settle their colonies in the Americas, especially in the Caribbean from the 1620s onwards, they turned – like the Spaniards, Dutch and Portuguese before them – to Africa for labour. As the British ferried Africans across the Atlantic into Barbados, Virginia and Jamaica, it was inevitable that more and more of them would find their way – mainly as slaves – to Britain. They landed in British ports as slaves, or as personal servants to captains, sailors and returning settlers and military officials. In this way the foundations were laid for the early black communities in Britain.

The largest black community in the eighteenth century was to be found in London, understandably since this was the nation's largest port with the most numerous trading links to the slave colonies and Africa. As Liverpool's participation in the slave trade grew, so black people also appeared in that port. But blacks were to be found across the face of Britain, in most cities and even in the remotest of rural spots. The landed classes, retreating to their country seats, took their black servants with them. Commentators frequently remarked on the black presence. In general, they were unskilled labouring people, most often employed as domestic servants. It is in that capacity that so many of them appear in contemporary paintings and pictures – part of the domestic scene in a stately home. But they were also used by artists to highlight the contrast between black and white.

Some were slaves. They were imported as slaves, were bought and sold as slaves. We can tell that more and more were brought to England because of the increase during the eighteenth century in advertisements for the sale of slaves or the recapture of runaway slaves in English newspapers. Indeed, they provide us with rare glimpses of individual slaves:

A healthy Negro Girl aged about fifteen years; speaks English, works at her needle, washes well, does household work, and has had the small pox. (*Daily Ledger* Dec. 31 1761)

To be disposed of. A Negro Boy of 12 years old, extremely well made, good-natured, sensible and handy, speaks English well, and has had the small Pox. Enquire at Mr Taylor's Barber's Shop, in Hart Lane, Covent Garden.
(*Daily Advertiser*, Feb. 11 1762)

Ran away from his Master, a Negro Boy, under 5 feet high, about 16 years old, named Charles, he is very ill made, being remarkably bow legged, hollow Backed and Pot-bellied; he had when he went away a coarse dark brown Linen Frock, a Thickset Waistcoat, very dirty Leather Breeches, and on his Head an Old Velvet jockey Cap. (ca.1768)

Runaway, some Time since, a negro lad about 18 years of Age, near five Feet two inches high, answers to the name of Starling, and blows the French Horn very well. (*British Journal*, 1757)

Ran away the first instant from Sir Phineas Pet at the Navy Office, a Negro about 16 years of age, pretty tall, he speaks English, but slow in speech, with a Livery of a dark coloured Cloth, lined with Blue, and so edged in the Seams, the Buttons Pewter, wearing a Cloth Cap, his Coat somewhat too short for him, he is called Othello.

There were, of course, a number of prominent, eye-catching black 'personalities' in Britain in the era of slavery. Billy Waters, 'King of the Beggars' (who lost a leg on a British warship), was buried with extraordinary popular pomp in 1823; Saartjie Baartman 'the Hottentot Venus' (a stripper who scandalized society); Bill Richmond and Tom Molineaux, the heavyweight boxers – these and others left their mark on the contemporary evidence.

But being a slave in Britain was different from being a slave in the slave colonies. First, it was unusual. In Jamaica, Barbados or Virginia slavery was the norm. In Britain it was wholly exceptional. In Britain, black slaves were surrounded by free people. Not surprisingly they often wanted to join them and to enjoy whatever benefits freedom had to offer. Some attempted to do so and, in London at least, a pocket of free blacks developed, keen to entice other slaves to join them – to run away and to leave their masters or mistresses for the uncertainties of freedom. Slave owners in England frequently complained of the free blacks who lured away their slaves.

English law was thrown into some confusion about their presence. Were they free in England – or were they slaves, like their contemporaries in the Americas? Throughout the eighteenth century English courts wavered, sometimes affording them the protection of the law, sometimes supporting their owners' claims that Africans were property – things – like slaves elsewhere. The property status of the black slaves in England was not finally resolved until slavery itself was abolished throughout British possessions in 1838.

The black community had its own favourite quarters and meeting places and its own distinct social life. In 1764 it was reported, for example, that 'no less than fifty-seven men and women, supped, drank, and entertained themselves with dancing and music, consisting of violins, French horns, and other instruments, at a public-house in Fleet Street, till four in the morning. No whites were allowed to be present, for all the performers were Blacks.'

When, in 1722, Lord Mansfield made his judgment that blacks could not be removed from England against their wishes, 200 local blacks gathered at 'a public house in Westminster to celebrate the triumph which their brother Somerset had obtained over Mr Stewart his master. Lord Mansfield's health was echoed round the room, and the evening was concluded with a ball. The tickets for admittance to this Black Assembly were 5s each.'

Most blacks in Britain were male and had domestic or poor labouring jobs, such as crossing sweepers. Some were beggars. After 1783, it was the poor blacks, especially those recently landed from North America, that caught the eye. To deal with these blacks, who had fought with the British against American independence, the government launched its ill-fated Sierra Leone scheme to repatriate them to Africa in 1787. It was significant, perhaps, that the official – and charitable – response to the development of a poor black

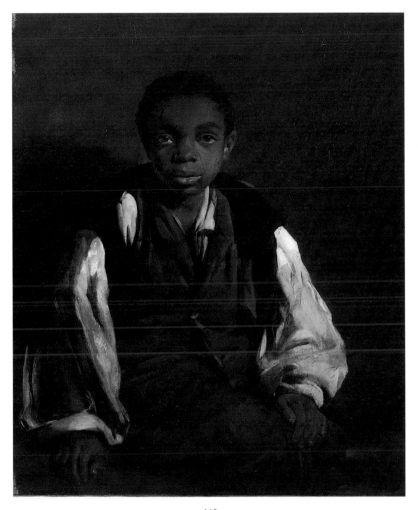

163
The Black Boy
About 1844, by William Windus (1822–1907), oil on canvas

community was to seek ways of shipping it out, ostensibly back 'home'. Of course, for most of the blacks involved Sierra Leone was not, and never had been, home. It involved not merely a leap in the dark, but a dangerous return to the region of West Africa where slave trading continued to thrive.

Like other poor people living on the margins of society, poor blacks were often ensnared in the punitive legal system. We often catch glimpses of them from their acts of desperation, and from the consequent legal punishments, which from 1788 included transportation to Australia.

By the middle years of the eighteenth century, a number of commentators began to complain about the number of blacks living in Britain, though they tended to inflate the numbers involved, if only to prove their case. In 1764 it was reported in *The Gentleman's Magazine* that 'the practice of

importing Negro servants into these kingdoms, is said to be already a grievance that requires a remedy, and yet it is everyday encouraged insomuch that the number in this metropolis only, is supposed to be near 20,000.'

Those who were most critical of the black presence were the West Indian planters and their friends. Yet it was often the planters, the slave traders and others who lived and worked in the slave colonies who brought slaves to Britain in the first place. This was a question which was more acutely debated after 1783, when the American slaves who had sided with the British in the recent War of American Independence came to Britain with their former masters.

What many of the West India lobby disliked was the fact that so many blacks were free. And even when, in principle, they were imported as slaves, many of them refused to

Fig.18
The Family of Sir William Young, ca.1766, by Johann Zoffany (Walker Art Gallery)
Young, seated with a cello, came from a plantation family in Antigua. He spent most of his time in England
despite holding appointments in the West Indies. His black servant is included in the group of figures.

accept their continuing bondage in Britain and simply ran away. They thus formed the basis for a black community which was prominent and readily visible in late eighteenth-century London.

But the black community had prominent friends – black and white – who, from the 1770s onwards, had raised the question of black freedom as a major social and political issue. The tide had begun to run against slavery, initially at least, within Britain itself. From the 1780s a number of black spokesmen lent their voices to the cause of black freedom, denouncing slavery in general and specifically in Britain. The publications of Equiano and Cuguano, and their letters and contacts, added to the growing concern about the existence of slavery in Britain itself. Indeed, it now seems clear that the early moves against slavery on a broader front began with a criticism of slavery in Britain.

Whatever the size of the black community, it evidently went into decline in the years after the ending of the slave trade in 1807. Thereafter, slaves were too valuable in the West Indies to be removed, for whatever reason, to Britain. Though other blacks settled in Britain in the early and mid-nineteenth century, the black community in the era of slavery was not to be matched in size or importance until later in the nineteenth century, when new shipping lines, especially to West Africa, helped to create new black communities in British ports such as Liverpool, London and Cardiff.[1]

Notes

1   Fuller accounts of the history of black people in Britain can be found in P. Fryer, *The History of the Black People in Britain*, London 1984; F. O. Shyllon, *Black Slaves in Britain*, Oxford 1974; and J. Walvin, *Black and White: The Negro and English Society, 1555–1945*, London 1973.

British Abolitionism, 1787–1838

JAMES WALVIN

At first sight, the British abolition movement was remarkably successful. Within twenty years of the movement's initial creation in 1787 the British Atlantic slave trade had been abolished. Later, when the movement had been reformed and revitalized after 1825, British slavery itself was abolished, between 1834 and 1838. No abolitionist in 1787 would have dared to hope that they would succeed so quickly and so thoroughly. But, of course, they were aided by forces they could scarcely understand, see or predict. What enabled the abolitionist movement to succeed were invisible forces transforming British life in conjunction with seismic changes among the slaves in the colonies. The abolitionist movement has, in large measure, been praised and rewarded for bringing the British slave system down. It is not to deny its importance – nor to minimize its crucial contribution – to claim that modern historians look for a much broader explanation for the end of the British slave system.

First, it is important to understand why abolitionists have received so much praise. The most prominent abolitionists (notably Thomas Clarkson and William Wilberforce) were great publicists, for themselves and their campaigns. Indeed it was part of their goal to establish in the British mind that they and their followers were the personification of the drive to end slavery. It was also an era which saw the unfolding of history in personal terms. This image, assiduously promoted by the powerful abolitionist propaganda machine, portrayed abolitionists as the good *versus* evil (slave owners). It provided an effective ploy. Moreover, after abolition in 1838, it was an image which was perpetuated by successive generations of nineteenth-century historians and commentators.

It is, of course, difficult to argue against that simplification without appearing to strip slavery of its gross immorality. And that, in a way, was a result of the work of the British abolitionists. What they did, quickly, unexpectedly and, in many respects, quite brilliantly, was to capture the high moral ground. Needless to say, the story was much more complex than that. Yet it needs to be stressed that the triumph of abolitionism helped to establish the abolitionists' own interpretation as *the* explanation for the ending of British slavery. The mythology of abolition lived on to become part of the accepted canon of British historiography. In the years since 1945, however, new views have prevailed.

The origins of the British abolition movement were rooted in the influence of Enlightenment writing (most notably Montesquieu) and the development of British non-conformity. The majority of men in the first abolitionist group in 1787 were Quakers. Quaker groups had been created across the face of Britain from the early eighteenth century, and they gave the founding abolitionists an immediate national network. They were also – and crucially – a literate constituency. Moreover many of these activists were influential and prominent men whose authority and status were unimpeachable and who could, accordingly, secure respect and a hearing in their locality.

This embryonic network was galvanized, like much else, by the impact of 1789. The vocabulary of abolition was transformed by the vernacular of the French Revolution. Of course those very changes, which sent a surge of energy and inspiration through British abolition, also served to fortify the resistance and determination of the British established order. If abolitionists and radicals viewed 1789 as a reason to press on with their reforms, defenders of the British regime took 1789 as added reason to dig in.

168
Patch box, with abolitionist motif, 'AM I NOT A MAN AND A BROTHER'
Enamel on copper, South Staffordshire, c.1790

171
One Penny Token, obverse: chained slave kneeling in supplication,
'Am I not a man and a brother', reverse: Whatsoever / ye would that /
men should do / unto you, do ye / even so to / them'
c.1790

173
Half-penny token, obverse: 'Am I not A Man And A Brother', reverse: clasped
hands, 'May Slavery & Oppression Cease Throughout The World'

Initially abolitionists were able to capitalize on the mood for reform by attracting remarkable numbers of signatures to abolitionist petitions which they submitted to Parliament. They issued cheap and plentiful tracts, simple publications which presented abolitionist arguments in a direct, crisp format to a British readership which was (at least in towns and cities) much more widespread than the government feared. We cannot tell how many people read this abolitionist literature. But we do know that it was consumed, in taverns, in coffee-houses, in private homes and in public meeting places, by the million.

The abolitionists' opponents – the West Indian planters, the Atlantic merchants and bankers and those with interests closely tied to the slave empire – were clearly taken by surprise. For more than a century they had thrived, unchallenged by questions of morality or economic utility, because they brought such amazing prosperity to Britain. Few could deny the wealth which flowed into the mother country. Whatever moral doubts may have existed, they remained the preserve of a minority. Moreover the incalculable suffering which the British slave empire had brought forth was far away in Africa, on the Atlantic crossings and in the slave colonies. There were, of course, thousands of Britons who knew what slavery really meant, most notably those men who worked on the slave ships and in the slave colonies, or those military and government officials who had spent part of their careers in the slave colonies. But they, too, stayed silent.

The slave lobby's case was simple and apparently irrefutable. The wealth which poured into Britain's major slave ports was massive and irreplaceable. Were the slave trade to end, it would bring the slave-based wealth of the Americas to a rapid conclusion. End the slave trade, they argued, and Britain would suffer massive economic loss.

For their part, the abolitionists adopted a different tack after 1787. Their basic premise was to attack the slave system of the Caribbean by ending the Atlantic slave trade. If Africans were no longer available to the planters – if they had to rely on existing slave populations for their labour force in the islands – the planters would be obliged to treat their slaves better. And if their treatment of slaves improved, the health of the population would improve, the population would flourish and, before long, a black peasantry would emerge which would provide the opportunity of free, rather than slave labour. It was, of course, a highly speculative venture. But it had the benefits of being specific and manageable.

Fig.19
Thomas Clarkson with his treasure-chest of samples of African produce and articles, painting by A.E. Chalon
Clarkson (1760–1846) was a founder member of the Society for Effecting the Abolition of the Slave Trade in 1787.

169
'African Hospitality', illustrating the verse 'Dauntless they plunge amidst the vengeful waves,/ And snatch from death the lovely sinking fair'
Engraved by J. R. Smith, after George Morland, 1 February 1791

From 1792, the abolitionists had lodged the issue of abolition inside Parliament. Thereafter it was subject to the whims and unpredictabilities of parliamentary moods and accidents. Indeed, had Wilberforce been a better manager of votes, it is very likely that Parliament would have passed abolition before 1807. There intervened, however, war between Britain and France, the revolution in Haiti and a domestic attack on British radicalism. From 1792 onwards, a growing body of opinion, inside and outside Parliament, feared demands for change because they seemed to be influenced by France and because they threatened to initiate the disasters which the French experienced in St Domingue. The slaves had begun to play an obvious and undeniable role in the debate about their own future. This was to be the turning point in the story of British abolition.

Initially, British MPs – and the propertied bodies which supported them – recoiled from the idea even of discussing the end of the slave trade because it seemed likely to threaten a reprise of events in Haiti. It seemed, they claimed, madness to debate abolition when in the Caribbean there was a convulsion among French slaves which threatened to prove contagious. Indeed planters throughout the region were deeply alarmed about the spread of slave insurrection from one island to another. The outcome was an effective end to realistic prospects for ending the British slave trade for a decade. Ultimately it took the ending of Pitt's regime and the brief period of peace between Britain and France before abolition made further headway. But when it did, in 1806, it rapidly passed through Parliament. By 1807 the British had ended their Atlantic slave trade.

170
'Slave Trade', illustrating the verse
'Lo the poor captive with distraction wild / Views his dear Partner torn from his embrace!'
Engraved by J. R. Smith after George Morland, 1 February 1791

Thereafter – indeed for more than a century – the British embarked on a new crusade: to persuade other participants in the trade to follow their own self-righteous lead. Having turned their backs on the slave trade, they sought to make others follow their example. Invoking morality and Christianity, but using the power of the Royal Navy and the diplomatic muscle of the Foreign Office, the British set about imposing abolition on the rest of the Atlantic world. Needless to say few people were impressed by this remarkable, almost St Paul-like conversion. Other European nations viewed it differently. The French doubted British sincerity, the Iberians still had empires which demanded fresh Africans and the new U.S.A. was unhappy to follow the lead of its former colonial governor. But this varied opposition did not deter the British from pursuing

what they regarded as their divinely appointed mission, to rid the Atlantic – indeed the wider world – of the scourge of the slave trade. Few of the British stood back to question the curiousness of their posture – slave poacher turned abolitionist game-keeper.

At the end of the European wars, the British used the Congress meetings to promote the case for international abolition, with varying degrees of success. They were also able to apply pressure through their ships and their diplomacy. Abolition in effect became a prominent aspect of British foreign policy for the rest of the nineteenth century. This international role caused intense irritation and grievance to other powers, most notably the French and Americans. The power of the British – buoyed up by expansive industrial wealth,

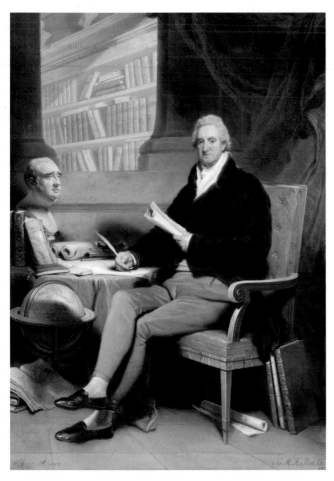

Fig.20
Portrait of William Roscoe (1753–1831)
Sir Martin Archer Shee, 1822, oil on canvas
Walker Art Gallery, National Museums Liverpool

182
Small cup with tropical scene and overseer
whipping a kneeling and chained slave
White china, printed in green, 19th century

reinforced by major international possessions, and implemented by a pre-eminent navy – masqueraded as a pious mission to safeguard virtue against the threats of evil. Opponents were more likely to see it in other terms.

British self-interest was no longer served by the slave trade. But if they sought to promote freedom, the new forms of economic prosperity that came with it suited, of course, a broad range of British interests. Freedom meant free trade, free labour, the free movement of capital, in effect the freedom of an ascendant British economy to invest, exploit and control – as best it could within the constraint of a new economic world system. Of course, this economic ideal had limitations. Nonetheless, it stood in marked contrast to the dominant ethos of the previous century. Freedom, not slavery, was the leitmotif of British Atlantic trade and business in the nineteenth century.

There was a brief respite, after the British abolition in 1807, before the abolitionists renewed their attack, on slavery itself. The gap was understandable. First, the war consumed all energies and diverted all demands for change. But, perhaps more important, it was essential to wait, to see what results were produced, in the islands, by the ending of the slave trade. By the early 1820s, when the first census returns from the slave islands had yielded their data (under the Registration Acts) it was clear that the slave population was in decline. This is exactly what planters had predicted. But it was merely a phase of a natural cycle, lasting only until young slaves, children when abolition was passed, entered their child-bearing years. From the mid-1820s the slave population began to pick up and grow, slowly but steadily. In the meantime, planters, faced with a possible decline in their slave labour force, began to reorganize their slave gangs. One result was that privileged slaves, and those who might have expected improvements, found themselves labouring in the fields. These reorganizations – necessary for the planters – served to increase discontent among the slaves.

There were other powerful forces for change among the slaves. First and foremost they were converting to Christianity, rapidly and universally in the British islands, notably to dissenting churches (Baptists and Methodists). With the end of the slave trade, more and more slaves were local-born as the Africans began to die out, and ever more of them were Christian. This had dramatic results which had long been feared by the planters but were generally unexpected by the missionaries. For a start it gave slaves an ideological unity which they had previously lacked.

180
Plate with abolitionist motifs and mottoes
White china, printed in brown, early 19th century

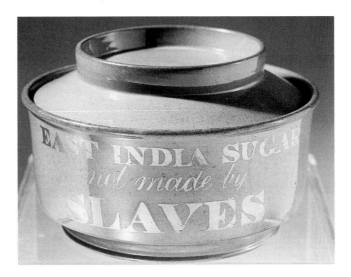

183
Sugar bowl
'East India sugar not made by slaves'
Stoneware, brown glazed, c.1822–34

185
Medal, obverse: 'Jubilee in Commemoration of the Abolition of Slavery in the British Colonies in the reign of William IV Aug 1 1834', reverse: freed man, woman and child, raising arms to heaven 'Give Glory To God'
T. Halliday, 1834

186
Medal, obverse: 'In commemoration of the extinction of colonial slavery throughout the British Dominions in the reign of William IV Augt 1 1834', reverse: freed man standing in sunlight holding broken chains, 'This is the Lord's Doing: It is marvellous in our eyes Psalm 118 v.23 JUBILEE AUGT 1 1834'
J. Davis, 1834

187
Medal, obverse: William IV seated beneath canopy attended by 4 statesmen (Lords Grey, Rusell, Brougham and Althorp) 'I advocate the bill as a measure of humanity', reverse: Seven people hands joined dancing around a palm tree, 'Slavery abolished by Great Britain 1834'
Bronze, probably by T. Halliday, 1834

More than that, it gave them a direct bond with a growing band of abolitionists in Britain. Non-conformists in Britain were outraged to hear stories about the punishments inflicted on their black co-religionists. Thus, in an unusual twist, black and white came together as never before.

It was in the Caribbean islands that black Christianity produced its most fundamental changes. First, the new chapels provided slaves with a meeting place away from the plantations. Chapel also offered a forum for the emergence of powerful black preachers, steeped in the imagery and vocabulary of the Bible. The Old Testament, in particular, was replete with imagery with direct relevance for people in bondage awaiting salvation and freedom. Black Christianity deeply impressed visitors to the islands with its fervour, its noise, its enthusiasms. But its most impressive impact remained unnoticed at first, for it was crucially important in focusing the slaves' attention on their condition and raising their hopes of salvation to come.

Black church leaders demanded a salvation in the here and now. More and more slaves were unprepared to wait for the distant prospects of heavenly salvation. Its most potent expression took the form of major slave rebellions, in Barbados in 1816, in Demerara in 1823 and then, most seismic of all, in Jamaica in 1831–32. The causes were local of course. But running like a descant through it all was a rising sense of unease, in Britain, about the processes needed to keep slavery in place. The question was asked: if slavery could only be kept in place by violence on a truly medieval level, was slavery worth it? Here we touch on the other crucial element in the fluctuating story of British abolition. Britain itself was changing.

By the mid-1820s the British had lurched into the first phases of major urbanization and industrial growth. A growing proportion of the people found themselves living in an urban habitat, where political organization was easier and where the printed word could circulate more freely and readily. Popular literature swirled through British towns as never before. For those who were interested, there were regular lectures on the abolitionist circuits. Tens of thousands turned up to listen to the abolitionist case. Indeed the only restraints on abolitionist lectures was the physical capacity of the meeting places. In all this women played an increasingly notable role. Thus, the printed and the spoken word swept up the British people in a well-orchestrated movement.

From 1825 abolitionists turned to the petition as an expression of opinion. MPs were lobbied in their

181
Comport with abolitionist motifs and mottoes
White china, printed in brown, early 19th century

184
Pair of figure groups, celebrating the end of slavery
Porcelain, painted in enamel colours, Staffordshire, c.1830–40

constituencies; they were in effect threatened that, unless they supported abolition in Parliament, abolitionists would direct their powerful armies of supporters against the MP in any future election. Thus a groundswell of abolitionist sentiment was built up, in the country at large and within Parliament. The process was completed in 1832 by the Reform of Parliament. Though they inaugurated a system still far from democratic, the reforms swept away many of the old pro-slavery MPs, replacing them with men in favour of abolition. The abolition campaign had yielded good returns in its attention to constituency politics.

Thus, after 1832, it was only a matter of time before the British Parliament decided to end black slavery. It was disliked at home, disliked in Parliament and, of course, was hated by its victims throughout the slave islands. It was not merely coincidental that Britain ended slavery at the moment it found its broader economic interests switching. By the late eighteenth century, it was clear to many commentators (most notably Adam Smith) that the restraints on trade necessary to support the old slave empire were ultimately damaging. The argument took a different form among the small-time investors and speculators who – for all the fabulous wealth normally associated with slavery – were the typical backers of the slave system. Men and women with spare cash to invest found that profits were higher, and certainly less speculative, in house-building or in local business investments, than in ships and slaves. It was not so much

that slavery became unprofitable, rather that other forms of economic activity were more attractive, less risky and more easily controlled.

Parliament brought slavery to an end, partially, in 1834. It was terminated in 1838 throughout British colonies. Thereafter, abolition became a key factor in that cultural imperialism which became the hallmark of the British for a century and more.

The temptation of modern scholars is to see the abolition of the British slave system merely as a function of broadly based economic and social changes in Britain and the Caribbean. In part this is a healthy antidote to the older school which thought in terms of personalities and religion. Yet there has been a danger, in recent years, of undervaluing the abolitionist movement, and its prominent leaders. In truth they played a crucial role, for they acted as a catalyst, capitalizing on those broader changes, often unconsciously. It was, after all, Parliament which abolished the slave trade and slavery. We need to know how and why that political change took place. The difficulty facing future historians is to explain the precise mix – the exact juncture – between the specifically political and the broad economic generalities. Though it seems doubtful that any future study will revert to an explanation focused on the abolitionists themselves, it would be wrong to marginalize them.

29
Plaque showing Bini figures
Brass, Benin, 16 / 17th century

The Impact of the Slave Trade on the Societies of West and Central Africa

PATRICK MANNING

Africa is a vast continent with a large population made up of many cultures and societies. It was far more than a reservoir from which enslaved people were taken. The influence of the Atlantic slave trade brought turmoil and redirection to the lives of many Africans. It transformed their societies and lives, brought about population decline, built new kingdoms and destroyed old ones. It created systems for the gruesome work of collecting and exporting slaves, and brought the expansion of a system of slavery in Africa itself. The experience of the Atlantic slave trade tied West and West Central Africa tightly to the Atlantic world, and laid the groundwork for Africa's weakness and dependency in the world of today.

The basic story of the trade in enslaved people from West and Central Africa is well documented, and experts are in wide agreement on its outlines. But new research results continue to appear. Scholars approach the same evidence with differing outlooks – they come, for instance, from Europe, the Americas and Africa. As a result, scholars are engaged in important disputes over both fact and interpretation of the Atlantic slave trade. Most of the debates centre on the question of how seriously African society was harmed by the Atlantic slave trade.

Africa's contacts with the wider world were new but not unprecedented. Before the European voyages, African societies had contacts with each other and, through long-distance trade routes, with the Mediterranean world, western Asia and the Indian Ocean. New contacts came as Portuguese and then other European voyagers opened the West Coast of Africa to ties across the Atlantic.

The era of the Atlantic slave trade covered, at its maximum, over 400 years from the mid-fifteenth century to the late nineteenth century. The changes in African life during the slave trade era are not a separate story or a sideline; they form one of the important elements in the story of the Atlantic slave trade as a whole.

In the first century or so of Atlantic contact, European visitors to Africa mostly sought gold and silver, and bought some spices. From the first, however, they also sought to capture and purchase slaves. European adventurers were always short of labour, and always seeking workers for agriculture and mining, and as servants and sailors. They sometimes captured and more often purchased captives along the African coast. This trade in chattel labourers gradually came to dominate all others. The slave trade impacted Africa at the margins of its society in the fifteenth and sixteenth centuries, but the patterns set in those early days grew to importance in the seventeenth century. During the eighteenth and nineteenth centuries the exploitation of Africa for captive labourers hit its most severe peak. The effects of the Atlantic slave trade on African life are still visible today.

The availability of some African captives for purchase by early Europeans shows that slavery existed, in certain forms, in Africa before the Europeans. The fact of early African slavery has sometimes led to confusion, or to arguments that Africans, because they held slaves, were somehow responsible for the extent to which slavery expanded during the era of the Atlantic slave trade. Rather than blame African victims or others, we should try to understand the operation of the whole Atlantic system and

28
Trumpet
Mande, Gambia

50
War trumpet
Ivory, Congo, 19th century

First, in Senegambia, Angola and the large kingdoms of Jolof and Kongo, the effects of the slave trade soon led to civil wars and disruption, which brought about the decline of the existing kingdoms on the one hand and the rise of new but smaller states on the other. One of the new states was the Portuguese colony of Angola, centred on the port of Luanda, from which Portuguese warriors and merchants exported several thousand slaves each year.

The second early pattern developed in Sierra Leone and nearby areas of the Upper Guinea Coast. In this region the slave trade proceeded more by kidnapping than by warfare. Some of the many captives were retained rather than exported, so that domestic enslavement, especially of women, expanded in the Upper Guinea Coast. While slavery expanded in the region, powerful states did not emerge.

In the seventeenth century, the sale of slaves grew so rapidly in the Bight of Benin that the region became known as the Slave Coast. Later in the same century some adventurers in the neighbouring Gold Coast found the rising prices of slaves so attractive that they gave up their interests in gold mining and trading in goods, and turned to the capture and export of slaves. In both of these areas, the wars accompanying the development of large-scale slave exports led to the creation of powerful states: Dahomey in the Bight of Benin and Asante on the Gold Coast.

The social transformations of these areas involved far more than the creation of powerful monarchies. The population of both regions, and especially of the Bight of Benin, declined for decades as a result of the continued warfare and export of slaves. In addition, since most of the captives sent across the Atlantic were male, these areas of the West African coast and its hinterland were left with a shortage of men. Many of the women who remained were now in slavery because of the wars. Women had to take on new tasks to sustain the economy, and the remaining men found it easier to take on second and third wives.

Slave exports from the Bight of Benin and the Gold Coast reached a peak about the 1720s, and declined somewhat thereafter – in part because the regional populations were now declining. Slave merchants then found new regions of the coast to draw into slave exports.

From the 1720s to the 1750s two forested regions without large kingdoms became the main new sources of slaves. These were the equatorial forest of the Congo (or Zaire) river basin, and the Bight of Biafra, populated especially by Ibo-speaking peoples. In both of these areas

its reliance on enslaved labour. The new system – the Atlantic slave trade and modern African slavery – became quite different from early African slavery. In the early days, war captives and other dependents who fell under the control of African rulers did the bidding of their owners. Since medieval times, a sizeable commerce across the Sahara had sent as many as 10,000 slaves in some years, mostly females, to serve masters in North Africa and the Middle East. But the number of persons held in slavery in Africa was small, since no economic or social system had developed for exploiting them.

After two or three centuries of the Atlantic slave trade, conditions in Africa had changed immensely. The 5,000 slaves purchased by the Europeans each year in the sixteenth century had risen to nearly 100,000 per year at the end of the eighteenth century. By the end of the nineteenth century perhaps five or six million persons were held in slavery on the African continent, many times more than could have been enslaved before the Atlantic slave trade began.

The initial European purchases of slaves disrupted society in limited areas of Africa. Waves of this influence then spread wider and grew more forceful. In the sixteenth century, two types of patterns emerged, depending on whether or not large states were involved in the slave trade.

Fig.21
Danish traders participating in an official ceremony with the Accras and Akuapems, from P. E. Isert,
Reise nach Guinea und den Caribäischen Inseln in Columbia, Copenhagen, 1788. Oto, a chief, is being installed as the Commander-in-Chief.
The Danes are seated at a table and the fort of Kongenstein at Ada, in south-eastern Ghana, can be seen in the background.

the demand for slaves and the rewards of selling them caused the development of new systems of delivering slaves. Slaves were captured primarily by individual kidnapping and by the sentencing of people to enslavement by court systems, following the earlier pattern of Upper Guinea. Through these devices, large numbers of people were taken to the coast and sold to European merchants, without, however, the formation of large kingdoms and massive raids of other parts of the continent. Perhaps the number of casualties was proportionately smaller in these areas. Nevertheless the export of people, besides the deaths due to exposure on long trips to the coast, was sufficient to cause the populations of each of these areas to decline for much of the eighteenth century and some of the nineteenth century.

In the Bight of Benin in the nineteenth century the rise of one great kingdom and the fall of another brought decades of warfare. The Sokoto Caliphate, a Muslim empire, rose just after 1800 to control all of what is today northern Nigeria and adjoining areas, and the neighbouring Oyo empire collapsed three decades later. These wars brought enslavement for hundreds of thousands, and deportation – to the Atlantic or the Sahara – for many of them.

Finally Angola, already one of the centres of slave exports two centuries earlier, was drawn after 1810 into exports on the greatest scale in the history of the Atlantic slave trade. Three state systems combined to collect captives and relay them to the coast: Portuguese-ruled Angola on the coast, Kazembe in the inland valleys and Lunda in the savannas of the far interior.

52
Map of Congo and Angola
John Ogilby, London 1670

These are some of the stories of the exports of slaves from Africa. But equally important are the stories of the changes in life for those who managed to remain in Africa.

After years of research and debate, scholars are now fairly well agreed on the number of people who underwent the Middle Passage: Paul Lovejoy's estimate of some twelve million persons loaded on ships at the African coastline is one most would accept. Far more difficult to agree, however, is the number of other Africans directly affected by the trade. This includes not only those who died on shipboard, but those who died during capture or during transportation within Africa, and the large number of enslaved people who remained in Africa or were traded to the Indian Ocean, Asia and North Africa. All agree that such a total is well beyond twelve million; research in progress may help reveal the details.

Where the slaves came from is also known in increasing detail. The regions of coast through which the greatest number of people passed were Angola, the Bight of Benin, Congo, and the Bight of Biafra, though other areas also lost large numbers of people. Debates continue on the ethnic origin of captives from each area of the continent, and on whether most captives came from near the coast or from the far interior. Recent research is showing that children became an increasingly important part of the Atlantic slave trade. One pattern is clear: while male slaves came from both the coast and the interior, female slaves came overwhelmingly from coastal areas. Women enslaved in the interior of Africa tended to be kept by African owners.

The overall size of the African population remains under debate. Views on the topic range from asserting that the slave trade had no effect on African population to estimating a drastic population decline. The most detailed recent research indicates a slow but steady decline in African population during the eighteenth and nineteenth centuries, an overall shortage of men, and local effects that were quite serious. The demographic losses due to slave trading consisted not simply in the numbers of persons

53
Map of Africa, printed and coloured
Probably from Ortelius, Theatrum Orbis Terrarum, Antwerp, 1570

sent overseas, but deaths in the course of capture and transport within Africa, and the loss of reproductive potential as young women were sent away.

The growth of slavery within Africa during the era of slave exports has become a major focus of research and debate. The dominant view is that slavery in Africa expanded through ties to the export slave trade, and remained important after the export trade declined. Slaves became most numerous in the parts of Africa where there were strong states, such as the Sokoto Caliphate, to keep them in submission, but slavery expanded to a lesser degree in such areas as the Congo basin and the Bight of Biafra where states were small. In Africa as in the Americas, some slaves escaped and formed maroon settlements. European conquest of Africa, in the years surrounding 1900, halted raiding for new captives but did not liberate those already enslaved. As late as the 1920s, millions of people in Africa had still not gained their freedom.

The impact of the slave trade on African political life has been complex and contradictory. From the earliest campaigns for abolition, a debate has raged on the question of whether the slave trade stimulated war in Africa. Those who say 'no' point to the stated war aims of participants in African wars, and note that the parties had other grievances and more specific objectives. Those who say 'yes' note the overall correlation between demand for slaves and the frequency of warfare. A parallel and unresolved debate continues between those who point out that the slave trade caused people to join in larger political units for protection, and those who emphasize that enslavement and greed caused the break-up of numerous states.

Similarly, the slave trade both created and destroyed fortunes in Africa. New social classes – of merchants, warlords and slaves – emerged in many areas of the continent. The export of slaves brought wealth to the African sellers, but very little of this wealth could be invested in expanding African production. Without slave exports, Africa would have had fewer imported goods, but would also have lost fewer productive labourers. As it was, many slaves were exchanged for various forms of money,

46
Plaque showing European with gun
Brass, Benin, 16 / 17th century

and one ironic result of the Atlantic slave trade is that it expanded the money economy in Africa. The result did not make the continent any richer. the consensus among scholars is that the slave trade was bad for African economies. The remaining questions are by how much, and how African societies were induced to participate in the downward spiral of slave trade. Research in progress on the prices of slaves in Africa and around the Atlantic will clarify these issues. It will also help answer the question of how much effect the British anti-slavery squadron had in suppressing the slave trade after 1808.

The long experience of the slave trade must have had a profound effect on the thinking of Africans. These patterns of thought are not yet well documented, but we can hint at them. Slavery and the slave trade seem to have brought contradictory experiences and contradictory ideas. On one hand it brought dreams of wealth and power, as seen in the great commercial city of Kano, the golden regalia of Asante, or the imposing royal statuary of Dahomey. On the other hand it brought the rejection of hierarchy and a strong desire for independence and equality. This egalitarian ideal is evident in the willingness of people to live in isolated villages to avoid submitting to slave raiders, and in the development of an artistic tradition, abstract in form, that emphasized ties to the ancestors and to such basic life forces as the earth. The position of women in African society today reflects both sides of this earlier choice: women play full and independent social roles, especially in commerce; yet the majority of slaves in Africa were women, and all women have suffered some oppression as a result. The widespread significance of divination (to learn the future) and common fears of witchcraft in Africa owe something to the uncertainty of life brought by centuries of slave trading. In these and other ways, the Atlantic slave trade changed the thinking of Africans.

Europeans conquered Africa in the years surrounding 1900. As the new rulers established direct control over African societies, and began to learn in detail about Africa, they often portrayed themselves as bringing about the first contact of Africans with the outside world. The reality was quite the contrary. Even though few Europeans had visited the African interior, West and Central Africa had been in close contact with the Atlantic world for 400 years already, and those contacts had grown more intensive with each succeeding century. Unfortunately, the contact was dominated by the Atlantic slave trade, with its corrosive effects for the peoples of the African continent.

47
Trade gun, known as a dane gun

48
Weights representing a) a man with gun, b) a gun, c) a cannon
Brass, Asante, Ghana, c.18th century

94
Flintlock blunderbuss
English, late 18th century

Fig.22
A procession of the Oba in the City of Benin, from Olfert Dapper, *Nauwkeurige Beschrijvinge der Afrikaansche Gewesten*, Amsterdam, 1668
The Oba or king is shown processing with a group of musicians and warriors with a view of the city of Benin in the background.

39
Kuduo, cylindrical base on cage-shaped stand
Brass, Asante, Ghana, c.1730–49

An African View of Transatlantic Slavery and the Role of Oral Testimony in Creating a New Legacy

MARY E. MODUPE KOLAWOLE

To the African, slavery in any form is considered to be one of the most dehumanizing and degrading aspects of human experience. The fact that African domestic slavery pre-dates transatlantic slavery does not change this position. Slavery is regarded in the African world-view as an undue intimidation and oppression of everyman by the royal class, or of the poor by the rich. Africans view the imposition of transatlantic slavery as an act that cannot be vindicated simply because slavery had existed, in one form or another, since before the time of the Roman empire. Jo Freeman highlights the long-standing existence of slavery in ancient European civilization and in particular, women's space in those societies: 'Roman law was an improvement over the Greek society. In that cradle of democracy only men could be citizens in the polis. In fact most women were slaves and most slaves were women ... In ancient Rome ... women and slaves could not assume proprietorship and in fact frequently were considered to be forms of property.'[1]

The nature of human interaction between African and European was inevitably conditioned by this existing social structure during the 'Age of Discoveries' of the fifteenth and sixteenth centuries when European exploration, maritime expertise and commercial activities increased in scope. Transatlantic slavery as a historical transaction has its origins in Portuguese exploration of the West Coast of Africa and their establishment of trading stations such as El Mina on the Gold Coast (Ghana). The Spanish and the Portuguese found the new West African routes useful alternatives to the East, enabling them to obtain spices directly, without the Arab middlemen. Africans then became involuntary participants. Some important decisions that were to affect Africa's very existence were taken without consulting the Africans. In 1494, the Treaty of Tordesillas, a precursor of the Berlin conference of 1884, shared out the world between Spain and Portugal, allocating Africa to Portugal.

Other Europeans – the French, the Dutch, the British and, to some extent, the Germans – followed suit. The tripartite trade became focused on African slaves as the most profitable commodity and source of wealth for the European plantation owners in the West Indies. Since Europeans and Indian indentured servants found the harsh, hot, tropical conditions unbearable, Africans who were used to such natural conditions became valuable assets to the plantation owners. They were generally treated as commodities with no human or legal rights. The enormity of the scope of transatlantic slavery and the level of human agony, as well as its impact and implication on the history of three continents, make it unique.

The plantation owners were not insensitive to the moral implication of the racially constructed transatlantic slave trade, and its obvious contradiction of Christian teachings and ideals. They were therefore quick in adducing various reasons and finding justification for their inhuman activity. Some Europeans argued that slavery already existed in Africa and that the transatlantic form

Fig.23
A coffle
Captives were marched, often in yokes, from the inland areas of Africa to the coast for sale to Europeans.

49
Yoke
West Africa, 19th century

provided better conditions and a chance to 'civilize' Africans. Some writers still try to validate transatlantic slavery to alleviate the sense of guilt. Many Western writers nonetheless document it with scholarly sincerity and integrity. It is, however, generally accepted that African slaves formed the backbone of European economic enrichment in the Caribbean colonies and contributed directly and indirectly to European economic and industrial growth.

African labour became indispensable and this accounts for the duration and continuous attraction of slavery. Inevitably, the transatlantic slave trade created an African Diaspora in Europe and the Americas. The consequences, in the creation of a new legacy and new racist ideologies, are ubiquitous, shaping several aspects of the lives of Africans, Europeans and Americans today. Many people believe that the wealth of cities such as Liverpool is inextricably linked to the transatlantic slave trade. In Africa, imperialism, colonialism and neo-colonialism became permanently entrenched in the mind, thought and experience of the people. The far-reaching consequences of these new alien concepts, ideologies and political structures determined the subsequent growth or diminishing of existing African civilizations, art, culture, architecture, education and technology.

Africans, however, attempt to revisit history through anthropological, archaeological, oral literary, oral historical and diverse other sources to objectify the experience and portray the transatlantic slave trade from the horse's mouth. To the African, the devastation suffered physically, psychologically, emotionally and morally almost defies atonement. Indeed, some of the socio-political problems that are peculiar to blacks in the Diaspora today take root in a scene of an omnipresent past and historical injustice. Although domestic slavery in Africa predates the transatlantic slave trade, it is essential to reiterate that there is a wide gap between the motive, nature, practice and implication of the two forms of enslavement. Domestic slavery was not racially constructed, nor did it involve the repugnant scope of degradation, geographical dislocation, cultural disorientation or forced acclimatization and attendant devastation and death.

African domestic slavery was characterized mostly by the rich, as well as powerful kings and chiefs, enslaving others. Slaves, therefore, included war captives, the kidnapped, adulterers and other criminals and outcasts. Every form of enslavement carries within it the germ of cruelty and degradation. But domestic slavery in Africa did not embrace the excessive dehumanization involved in the new form of enslavement. Palace chiefs in many parts of Africa, though slaves, enjoyed certain privileges that were envied by lower-class and poor free people. Royal slaves of the Alafin of Oyo and Ooni of Ife were highly regarded because they had privileged access to the king and could even seek favours from him. They sometimes enjoyed relative affluence and a prestigious position, like those of Ilari slaves (slave officials). Odi slaves in Ijebu palaces were known to have a special status as well.

African women's peculiar degradation in transatlantic slavery

In traditional African slavery, women slaves were often domestic hands to the rich and they enjoyed a better condition of life than some free women. Women leaders such as Madam Tinubu of Abeokuta and Lagos as well as Queen Amina of Zaria had many female slaves. Although malestream documents present them as cruel rulers, a female Ooni of Ife, Olowu, used slaves productively for making terraced roads invented by using local pottery pieces. These can still be seen in some parts of Ile-Ife today.[2] Another form of domestic slavery was the Iwofa or *iwefa*, a means of holding people as a ransom until a debt was redeemed. This was a transient and conditional form of enslavement. In many parts of West Africa, slaves could redeem themselves and earn their freedom.

The transatlantic slavery, however, brought an indescribable level of agony and unprecedented quest for enslavement because of the increasing desire for European goods such as alcohol, tobacco, firearms and other items. Forced and more permanent separation and harrowing tumultuous experience followed, as people, usually youthful, robust men and women at the most productive age, were extracted and uprooted from their family, friends and fatherland. In all this, women as mothers felt the agony more profoundly. The lure of better conditions in Europe and the Americas was not justified by attendant emotional, physical and psychological trauma and dehumanization. Women often had their children kidnapped and enslaved in their absence while slave women were often separated forcibly from their enslaved children.

The transatlantic slave trade brought new levels of degradation and suffering to women because the intensified attraction of European goods made Africans more greedy to acquire slaves. The availability of European firearms

16
Comb
Carved wood, Old Calabar, Nigeria

17
Robe
Woven indigo-dyed cotton embroidered with white cotton, Hausa, Nigeria

25
Calabash guitar with bow
West Africa

26
Small drum with drum stick
West Africa

intensified inter-tribal and intra-tribal wars, especially as more prisoners of war meant more slaves and more firearms. Africans became hardened and women received the butt-end of this callousness. Men married more wives to produce more children, a ready source for the slave market! Some African slave owners were more eager to sell female slaves off to Europeans as they kept male slaves for agricultural and professional roles such as palace drummers. Between 1724 and 1727, King Agaja of Dahomey sold large numbers of female slaves before the loss of Ouidah (Whydah) curtailed his trade.[3] An understanding of African women's exaltation of motherhood and mothering will depict the intensity of the African woman's agony during this nadir of human degradation. Women's dignity and self-esteem were violated during slavery and the subsequent Middle Passage and it continued till the post-bellum period in the Diaspora.

African women's resistance and resilience
The erroneous impression is often created that African women took enslavement, like subjugation and subordination, for granted as a normal fact of their reality and so did not resist transatlantic slavery. On the contrary, documents show us that they resisted European subjugation just like men. Slave revolts, insurrections in Africa, *en route* and on the plantations in the Diaspora did

not exclude women. Women were involved directly or indirectly in resistance against King Afonso I in the Congo (1529), Guinea slave traders (1556), in Sao Tome (1560) and the Macingo rebellion (1570).

African warfare between the sixteenth and the nineteenth centuries depended largely on metaphysical and psychological aspects and women were indispensable in these. Yet African women's roles were not adequately documented until recent research on women's resistance in the pre-colonial, colonial and post-colonial periods.[4]

Many European explorers, historians and colonial administrators have given subjective and inaccurate accounts of women's docility and lack of resistance. Thomas Winterbottom wrote: 'In Africa, women are regarded as beings of an inferior nature, and as born to be the slaves of men ...'[5] Ironically, he portrays the Mandingo slave revolt in Sierra Leone (1785–86) which was not an all-male uprising.

African female forms of resistance included poisoning slave owners or contaminating their food. Others adopted mystic curses that were believed to be potent and at least frightened some slave owners if invoked by an angry slave. Others even tried to escape or commit suicide as an alternative to degradation and dehumanization. Revolts in slave warehouses at El Mina castle, Goree, Luanda, Zanzibar and Mombasa cut across gender lines. The acme of slave women's revolt, resistance and resilience is seen in the role of the Amazon warriors in Dahomey, who consisted largely of female slaves. They were crucial to the attacks and plundering of European slave forts and factories. Women also constituted a formidable force in attacks on baracoons.

In Dahomey, under King Agaja, women slaves dominated the army and they were crucial in the protective role of frontier guards. They resisted local incursions from neighbours like the Egbas as well as European slave traders. King Behazin's one thousand wives were central to the resistance against the Germans, although he was later captured. The Amazon warriors, consisting largely of women slaves, were always troublesome to captors. Eight thousand Amazons resisted Beecroft in 1851.[6] According to Hosen Joffe, organized resistance in various parts of Africa retarded slavery: 'Resistance saved whole villages untold millions of lives, engineered many escapes, frightened off many slaving expeditions ...'[7] Women acted as motivators where they were not activators. They also took part in predatory expeditions and slave conspiracies and insurrections.

The role of oral literature and history and the creation of a legacy

Oral literature and history play an important role in highlighting the nature of the experience of slavery, of resistance and the creation of a new legacy in the African Diaspora. Some measure of cultural continuity was achieved through oral tradition and language. Women played a vital role in their preservation and they deployed oral poetry, folk-tales and anecdotes to create an African cultural base that is, for example, the prototype of the Brer Rabbit and Uncle Remus tales. Cultural transmission was an effective tool of resilience and resistance as slaves refused to allow the trauma to destroy their identities completely.

Women used oral as well as written poems, songs, folk-tales, proverbs, anecdotes, parables and fables to transpose African culture to the new world as well as relive their African experience. This oral genre pre-dated the slave narratives by Olaudah Equiano and others. It was also antecedent to works by modern writers such as Zora Neale Hurston, Ralph Ellison, Edgar Wright, Maryse Conde, Alice Walker and others.

There are many aspects of transatlantic slavery that have remained controversial. Generally, Africans focus on the indescribable, even irreparable, damage and trauma caused by this peculiar human interaction. Eurocentric scholars attempt to vindicate or provide an apologia, while theorizing about the normalcy of slavery and its indigenous nature in Africa. Africans in the Diaspora continue to seek a meeting point between their African heritage and the inevitable reality that they have come to stay in the Diaspora and have acquired new sets of values which must necessarily be properly integrated. This paradox of cultural identity in a multi-cultural setting continues to inform the search for new directions. Cultural enrichment through literature, music, dance, the arts, fashion and cookery, among other activities, are aspects of European and American realities today.

Women of African origin in the Americas and the Caribbean play a leading role in the search for meaningful relocation and empowerment in the new multi-cultural setting of the Diaspora. There has been an increase in the quest for a new identity in a move to explore the past, especially the transatlantic slave trade, to explicate the present and carve new positive paths for the future. These women tell their stories without self-pity while exploring African arts, literature, folklore, philosophy, fashion, religion, even cookery, to recreate their African heritage

22
Bow lyre
Leather, wood and string, West Africa

and experience. The new quest for cultural discovery and recovery in the last half of the twentieth century is a direct result of the role of women in transmitting African values through story-telling, poetry, song and dance, *inter alia*.[8]

In her research into African legacy in the Caribbean, Maureen Warner-Lewis (she adopted the Yoruba name Morenike) identifies the centrality of music, oral poetry, literature and oral history in 'stimulating and sustaining memory'.[9] She recorded about 150 songs in the Yoruba language that are still actively sung by Trinidad elders. Many of her informant-singers are women. These relics from the past emphasize the survival of African culture largely due to women's resilience. Much Trinidadian oral poetry still reveals Yoruba metaphor, form and world-view today.[10] The minor-key calypso is believed to have considerable Yoruba influence as well, and this is true of other literary and artistic forms by Africans in the Diaspora.[11] One can conclude that apart from positive legacies, some contemporary problems such as racism are legacies of the transatlantic slave trade that the world continues to confront.

Notes

1. Jo Freeman, 'The Building of the Gilded Cage' in Ann Koedt *et al.*, *Racial Feminism*, New York, Quadrangle, 1973, p. 129.
2. David Sweetman, *Women Leaders in African History*, Oxford, Heinemann, 1984.
3. I. A. Akinjogbin, *Dahomey and Its Neighbours, 1708–1818*, Cambridge, Cambridge University Press, 1967.
4. Nina Emma Mba, *Nigerian Women Mobilised*, Berkeley, University of California, 1982.
5. Thomas Winterbottom, *An Account of the Native Africans*, vol. 1, London, Frank Cass, 1969, ch. ix, pp. 144–54.
6. Saburi Biobaku, *The Egbas and Their Neighbours*, Oxford, Clarendon Press, 1965, pp. 34ff.
7. Hosen Joffe, *A History of Africa*, New Jersey 1885, p. 48.
8. bell hooks, *Yearning, Race, Gender and Cultural Politics*, Boston MA, Southend Press, 1990; Leonard Dinnerstein *et al.*, *Natives and Strangers. Blacks, Indians and Immigrants in America*, New York, Oxford University Press, 1990.
9. Maureen Warner-Lewis, *Guinea's Other Suns*, Dover MA, The Majority Press, 1991.
10. *Ibid.*, pp. 98–101.
11. *Ibid.*, pp. 144–47.

Racist
Ideologies

STEPHEN SMALL

I am apt to suspect the negroes and in general all other species of men, to be naturally inferior to the whites. There never was a civilised nation of any complexion than white nor even any individual eminent in action of speculation. No ingenious manufacturer among them, no arts, no sciences. There are negro slaves dispersed all over Europe of which none ever displayed any symptoms of ingenuity. (David Hume, 1734)[1]

Vices the most notorious seem to be the portion of this unhappy race; idleness, treachery, revenge, cruelty, impudence, stealing, lying, profanity, debauchery, nastiness and intemperance, are said to have extinguished the principles of natural law, and to have silenced the reproofs of conscience. They are strangers to every sentiment of compassion and are an awful example of the corruption of man left to himself.
(*Encyclopaedia Britannica*, 1810, vol. xiv, p. 750)[2]

... there is a physical difference between the white and black races which I believe will forever forbid the two races living together on terms of social and political equality. And inasmuch as they cannot so live, while they do remain together there must be the position of superior and inferior, and I as much as any other man am in favor of having the superior position assigned to the white race.
(Abraham Lincoln, 1858)[3]

Definitions of 'racism'

'Racism' has been defined in a number of different ways. In the past most discussions focused on the development by Europeans of ideologies that argued that Africans and Europeans were separate 'races', endowed with different physical and mental attributes, and that Europeans were superior and Africans inferior. The accepted scientific view today dates from a UNESCO statement of the 1940s: 'Racism falsely claims that there is a scientific basis for arranging groups hierarchically in terms of psychological and cultural characteristics that are immutable and innate'.[4] One of the problems with discussions of 'racism' is that some people use the term to refer to the content of an ideology (regardless of any actions that do or do not follow); others mean it to refer to the intentions of individuals or groups; still others refer to the outcomes of actions, intended or otherwise (as in institutional racisms); still others use it to mean all of these. For example, the Institute of Race Relations declares: 'Racialism refers to prejudiced beliefs and behaviour but when these become fully systematised into a philosophy of "race" superiority, and when this then becomes a part of the way in which society as a whole is organised, then we use the term racism. An individual who acts in a racially prejudiced way is a racialist; a society whose most powerful economic and social institutions – industry, law, media, government – are organised on, or in effect act on, the principle that one "race" is superior to another is racist.'[5]

A second problem is that there has often been a futile search for the origin of 'racism', a search that suggests that there is a single 'racism' with a single origin. This is characteristic of the view that 'racism' began with slavery in the Americas. This notion has now been discredited

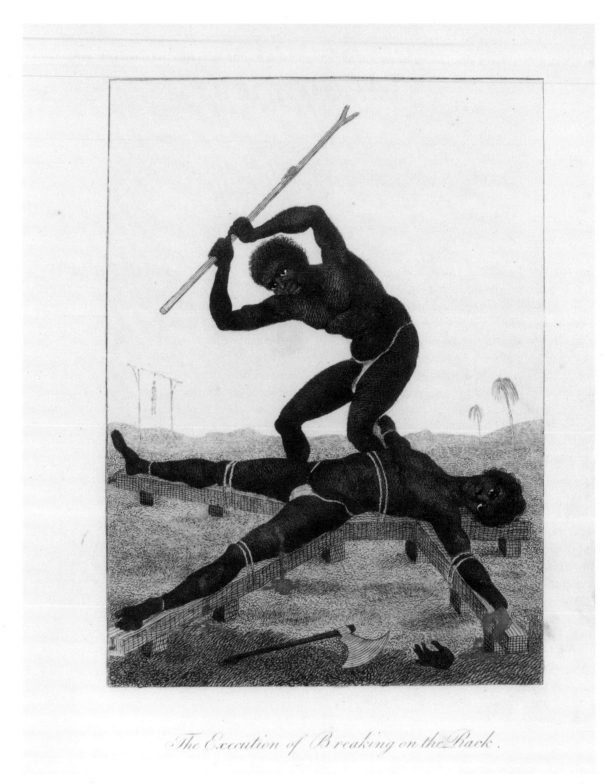

The Execution of Breaking on the Rack.

Fig.24
'The execution of a slave, Surinam, 1792' from J. G. Stedman, *Narrative of a five year expedition against the Revolted Negroes of Surinam*, 1772–77, London 1796
Slaves were often forced to inflict punishment on one another and such images helped to reinforce European racial prejudices. Here a free carpenter named
Neptune is being executed for killing an overseer.

and it is clearly better to conceptualize different 'racisms', and to recognize that ideologies can reflect different 'racist' assumptions.

Another complicating factor is the idea that 'racism' is simply one form of ethnocentrism and that ethnocentrism has occurred in all societies at all times. This suggests that racism is thus no better and no worse than other ethnocentrisms. This neglects the way in which racism towards Africans during slavery has been both more pernicious and lasting in its effects. This 'racism' is inextricably intertwined with financial accumulation, economic expansion, industrial acquisition and the rise and development of capitalism; the international contours of economic, political and social instability reflected in present-day world trade; the enduring effects of racial group barriers, boundaries and identities in the colonial and post-colonial world; the creation of current nation states (both inside and outside Europe) and current national configurations and conflicts in Africa; advances in science which were seized upon to 'justify' oppression and exploitation and injustice; mass voluntary and enforced migrations that populated (and depopulated) the Americas, and has led to the Diasporic presence throughout Europe; the realities of citizenship and non-citizenship, and the extension or denial of the inalienable right to life, liberty and the pursuit of happiness; the cultures and communities of African resistance, from the advocates and practitioners of black Nationalism to those of PanAfricanism, including Martin Delany, Marcus Garvey, W. E. B. Dubois and Kwame Nkrumah.

The enduring effects of 'racism' today are unique to the Atlantic slave era and its effects are almost palpable across the world. This makes it more significant and widespread and its impact more immediate.

Historical changes in ideas about 'race'

It is a mistake to assume that 'racisms' were constant over time, or in different places at the same time. Most of the evidence indicates that early European views of Africans were articulated in religious rather than 'racial' terms. Over time, particularly as slavery became entrenched and was presumed indispensable to European needs, the language of 'racism' became more and more explicit. Winthrop Jordan[6] has documented the changing language used to refer to people from Europe and Africa. The first English to 'settle' in North America called themselves 'Christians' and called Africans 'Negroes'. In the middle of the seventeenth century they increasingly called themselves 'English' and 'free'; after the 1680s they called themselves 'white'.

Banton[7] has shown the development of the language of 'race' both in Europe and in the Americas and he argues that there is no evidence that the word 'race' was used at all in the Americas to differentiate Europeans and Africans until after 1776. The word first appeared in Europe before any contact with Africans, and it referred to lineage, or likeness, without any notion of biological immutability. Relationships of superiority and inferiority are only implied, or are articulated around cultural not biological difference. Thus one has the Irish race, English race and so on. At this time, the word simply refers to a group with common origins. This remained the primary meaning of the word during the sixteenth, seventeenth and eighteenth centuries, and in its applications to Europeans.

As contacts with Africans persisted, most European scientists and middle-class Europeans came to believe that there were three basic races – Caucasoids, Negroids and Mongoloids. While European and (white) American scientists differed greatly on the number of races, they all shared the common (and mistaken) assumption that distinct and unequal races existed. The common mistakes and futility of it all are summed up by Gossett: 'Linnaeus had found four human races; Blumenbach had five; Cuvier had three; John Hunter had seven; Burke had sixty-three; Pickering had eleven; Viry had two "species", each containing three races; Haeckel had thirty-six; Huxley had four; Topinard had nineteen under three headings; Desmoulins had sixteen "species"; Deniker had seventeen races and thirty types.'[8] For some scientists, 'the idea of race was so real that no amount of failure could convince them that it might be an illusion'.[9]

Numerous European and European-American scientists claimed to offer scientific evidence about racial difference, including many of the most notable and eminent scholars of their day. Their work is usually called 'scientific racism'. They include (in the eighteenth century) George Louis Leclerc Buffon and Johan Friedrich Blumenbach in Europe, Dr Charles White in England, and the Reverend Smith in the United States; and (in the nineteenth century) James Cowles Prichard in England, Baron Cuvier and Geoffroy Saint-Hilaire in France, Dr Samuel George Morton, Josiah Clark Nott and George Robin Gliddon in the United States. Blumenbach is responsible for the division of the races into Caucasian, Mongolian, Ethiopian, American and Malay, corresponding to white, yellow, black, red and brown. He may have coined the word 'Caucasian' to mean whites.[10]

When Darwin wrote his *Origins of Species* he fundamentally changed the scientific basis for thinking about race and race differences. But though European scientists eventually accepted his arguments about the basis of human differentiation – that there were multiple overlapping differences between humans, with as many differences within presumed races as between them – they simply modified their racism to suit these new findings.

It is usually assumed that the conclusions of 'scientific racism' were based on the best systematic scientific principles at the time. This is where there is confusion with the idea of 'pseudo-science': 'science' referring to established and accepted principles of the academy, 'pseudo-science' referring to rejected and unacceptable principles. It has become clear that much of the evidence was deliberately distorted and conflicting evidence was ignored. Similarly, the evidence was unconsciously distorted as a result of the unquestioned assumption that European culture was unassailably superior to all others. In any case, Blumenbach's characterization of whites as Caucasian – a classification which still stands even today in the United States and Britain – is based on the observation of a single skull.[11]

Despite proclaiming objectivity, impartiality and openness to all evidence and views, it is clear that none of the dominant studies of racism invited or allowed Africans to offer scientific contributions.

Ideologies of race and gender

While racisms were applied to all Africans, it is clear that distinctions were drawn between men and women as objects of exploitation and manipulation. Europeans were obsessed with African sexuality from the start and different ideologies were developed about African men and African women. Black men were seen as rapists to be lynched and black women as sexual objects to be raped. These ideologies reflected and reinforced the power of gender relations within the white population. All of this served to justify (in Europeans' minds, especially men) their own desires, anxieties and frustrations. It helped ease the conscience of Europeans about breeding, using black men as 'studs', as well as about raping and abusing African women.

In general, 'Whites viewed white women as chaste and pure, charged with the task of ensuring that white men remained "civilized", while whites saw black women as natural whores who enticed white men into sexual relationships'.[12] Davis maintained the central facet of domination was pragmatism: 'Expediency governed the slave holders' posture toward female slaves: when it was profitable to exploit them as if they were men, they were regarded, in effect, as genderless, but when they could be exploited, punished and repressed in ways suited only for women, they were locked into their exclusively female roles'.[13] Women thus worked in slave fields, in coal mines, in iron foundries or as lumberjacks and ditch-diggers. Nor did pregnancy exempt them from such work.

During slavery 'black women's bodies were ... the playing fields where racism and sexuality converged. Rape as both right and rite of the white male dominating group was a cultural norm'.[14] Furthermore, 'rape was a weapon of domination, a weapon of repression, whose covert goal was to extinguish slave women's will to resist, and in the process, to demoralize their men'.[15] And yet this convergence is the least researched, even in the 1990s, of all the areas of slavery. Consequently, says hooks, there are no books on the 'sexual sado-masochism of the master who forced his wife to sleep on the floor as he nightly raped a black woman in bed'.[16] This sexual abuse has always been all but glossed over in most literature.[17]

Benign racism

We should not assume pro-slavery whites were all racists and abolitionists were all anti-racist. For example, many slave masters believed blacks were human but they were not prepared to forego their profits from slavery, while many abolitionists believed slavery was evil, that blacks were human, but they were not prepared to interact with them on a social level of equality, certainly not in the area of sexual relations and marriage. None doubted that whites were superior.

Some white abolitionists felt sorrow for Africans, others saw them as the means to rectify the impurities in the white 'race'. For example, many felt that Africans had greater 'religious tendencies', greater 'strength of attachment' and 'gentility' from which the whites could learn. Such benevolent reformers, even romantics, 'tended to see the Negro more as a symbol than as a person, more as a vehicle for romantic social criticism than as a human being with the normal range of virtues and vices'.[18] An example is William Ellery Channing, a moderate anti-slavery writer, who in *Slavery* of 1835 argued 'the African is so affectionate, imitative, and docile that in favourable circumstances he catches much that is good; and accordingly the influence of a wise and kind master will be seen in the very countenance of his slaves'.[19]

Furthermore, many abolitionists refused to let black children into their schools, or to employ blacks except as menials. Some claimed this was dictated by the pressures of the times, but for many it revealed clear antipathies.

A major dispute about the roles of black people in the abolitionist movement in the United States led Frederick Douglass to campaign on his own. White abolitionists had paraded Douglass in front of northern audiences as an example of the adverse effects of slavery on black people. They encouraged him to stutter, act dazed and roll his eyes. But despite being enslaved, Douglass was an accomplished intellect and orator. Fed up of acting out the role of a poor pathetic ex-slave he wanted to contribute more intellectually and analytically to the movement. He was strongly dissuaded and for him, enough was enough. He began to campaign independently of white abolitionists.

Influences on 'racist' attitudes

In general, 'racist' ideas reveal more about the motives and insecurities of whites than about the characteristics or attributes of blacks. A combination of material interests (economic, political and psychological) as well as cultural beliefs gave rise to 'racist' beliefs. Some analysts see such beliefs arising from religious convictions – the idea that blacks were the descendants of Ham described in the Bible. In this conception Christians were simply bringing heathens to be saved in the bosom of the Lord, and slavery was represented as a 'rescue mission'.

Other analysts believe that 'racism' arose from exaggeration and myth about Africa and Africans who were enslaved. For example, stories, tales and caricatures about Africa and Africans were available, or could be interpreted, from the Bible, classical and medieval accounts – *Mandeville's Tales* was a prime example. From the 1570s there was 'an outpouring of literature on Africa'.[20] These accounts described the geography, people, animals and climate of Africa in a colourful and bizarre style such that 'fact and fiction became inextricably fused'.[21] Many such tales were clearly distorted and exaggerated to enhance the stature of the person telling them to audiences that were usually illiterate and gullible. The importance of these early tales is that they set the backdrop for all future understanding of Africa and 'truth fed the expansion rather than the expulsion of mythology, and rumour unshakably fastened itself on reality'.[22]

138
Punishment collar
Wrought iron, 18th century

For still others, 'racist' beliefs arose from personal experience and familiarity with Africans as subordinates. This was the case throughout the Americas for slave masters and non-slave-holding whites. Having forced Africans into slavery, having imposed inferiority by denying them means or motivation to read and write, and having established a system whereby all values, traditions, achievements and accomplishments were to be judged by European values and morality, there was little that the African could do not to be inferior, at least in the eyes of Europeans. This is clearly tied in with 'racism' as cultural arrogance.

One of the main explanations for the origin and growth of 'racist' ideas is the view that they arose primarily from the economic and political needs of Europeans, especially those with power, who sought to maximize the profits from the colonization of the Americas. Most notable is the contention of Eric Williams that 'slavery was not born of racism: rather, racism was the consequence of slavery'; and that the reason for slavery 'was economic, not racial; it had to do not with the colour of the labourer, but the cheapness of the labour'. Williams demonstrated how working-class whites, Native Americans and others were first used as sources of labour, but that Africans were identified as being economically cheaper, available in greater numbers and with fewer (military) repercussions for the Europeans.[23] Over time, the fact that Africans were overwhelmingly slaves gave a 'racial twist' to slavery, and Europeans came to assume that it was the 'natural' position for Africans. This is a view shared by Walvin: 'The first wave of white expansion into Africa ... was conceived in the commercial dreams of European speculators and born of shrewd investment' rather than being about religious liberation.[24]

There is evidence to show that all these sources exercised some impact on 'racist' views. Sometimes it is clear that one particular source was more important than others, though it was often the case that many different sources came together. It seems unlikely that one source alone was the primary force at all times, and it is thus better to ask when and where each source was important, and for which groups. Miles has argued that, though many of these influences were significant, they all became secondary to the economic and political motivations of the dominant groups in the European nations.[25] As the fortunes and prosperity of the European nations became so intertwined with the exploitation of Africa and the Americas, the issue of whether, in truth, black people were inferior or not became almost irrelevant. The belief in their inferiority by Europeans suited their economic and political pursuits; if it had been advantageous to believe they were equal or even superior, then Europeans would have adjusted their beliefs. In fact they did, for it was clearly believed that Africans were superior workers.

Working-class whites accepted 'racist' views because it supported them psychologically and it provided economic incentives. It enabled them to feel superior to someone, and it left them with the possibility of becoming slave masters themselves some day. Thus a Georgia song popular among working-class whites runs: 'All I need in this creation is a pretty little wife and a slave plantation'.

Notes

1. Peter Fryer, *Staying Power: The History of Black People in Britain*, London, Pluto Press, 1987.
2. James Walvin, *Black and White: The Negro and English Society, 1555–1945*, London, Allen Lane, 1973.
3. Michael Banton, *The Idea of Race*, London, Tavistock, 1977.
4. Ashley Montagu, *Statement on Race*, London, Oxford University Press, 1972, p. 158.
5. Institute of Race Relations, *Patterns of Racism*, London 1982, p. 28.
6. Winthrop Jordan, *White Over Black. American Attitudes Toward the Negro, 1550–812*, New York, W.W. Norton and Co., 1968.
7. Banton, *op. cit.*
8. Thomas Gossett, *"Race". The History of an Idea in America*, Schocken 1965, p. 82.
9. *Ibid.*, p. 83.
10. *Ibid.*, p. 37.
11. *Ibid.*, p. 38.
12. Theresa L. Amott and Julie A. Mattei, *Race, Gender and Work*, Boston, South End Press, 1991.
13. Angela Davis, *Women, Race and Class*, The Women's Press, 1981, p. 6.
14. bell hooks, *Yearning. Race, Gender and Cultural Politics*, Boston, South End Press, 1990, p. 57.
15. Davis, *op.cit.*, p. 24.
16. hooks, *op.cit.*, p. 57.
17. Davis, *op.cit.*, p. 25.
18. George Stocking, *Race, Culture and Evolution*, New York, Free Press, 1968, p. 109.
19. *Ibid.*, p. 103.
20. Walvin, *op.cit.*, p. 22.
21. *Ibid.*, p. 5.
22. *Ibid.*, p. 6.
23. Eric Williams, *Capitalism and Slavery*, North Carolina 1944.
24. Walvin, *op.cit.*, p. 16.
25. Robert Miles, *Racism and Migrant Labour*, London, Routledge, *1982*; idem, *Racism*, London, Routledge, 1989.

On the Meaning and History of Slavery

PRESTON KING

What does slavery mean?

Slavery always involves compelling some to work for others. But it comes in many forms and degrees. It is very broadly conceived when used to cover any form of compulsory labour. It is more commonly conceived narrowly, to cover only those workers denied all legal or civic rights. The actual conditions of life and work for slaves, however expressed in law, vary in important ways from one town or region or country to another.

What are the different forms of slavery?

Scholars vary in their approaches. There are many different classificatory schemes, no one of which is really adequate. Below, I recommend a rough working distinction between comprehensive and restrictive meanings of slavery.

1. Slavery, in the comprehensive sense, may be taken to involve compulsory labour of any kind – whether for a specific purpose (perhaps to drain a swamp), or for a fixed term (perhaps for five years, after which liberty is restored), or for a recurrent duty (perhaps to reap a harvest on behalf of another). Thus conceived, slavery may refer to such diverse arrangements as Russian serfdom, European medieval villeinage and Spartan helotry (the tenant is tied to the land); the Ottoman janissary corps (Turkish infantrymen, of the fourteenth to nineteenth centuries, compelled to serve for life); English 'statutory service' (forcing the poor in the sixteenth and seventeenth centuries to submit and work for domestic masters);[1] impressment into the army; 'shanghai-ing' into the navy; compulsory transportation (as to seventeenth-century Virginia and eighteenth-century Australia); convict labour (as in pre-1776 Georgia, in post-1788 New South Wales, in the Soviet 'Gulag Archipelago' and widespread everywhere); 'chain-gang'

labour (as in the twentieth-century U.S. South); indentured labour (as of East Indians to Guyana, Trinidad and Fiji in the nineteenth century); child labour (as in so much of the carpet industry in India, Bangladesh and Pakistan); and child prostitution (as currently in Thailand, the Philippines and elsewhere). All of these are cases of unfree, dependent or compulsory labour.

2. Slavery is more commonly conceived in the restrictive sense, involving compulsory labour which is unrelieved by any legal restrictions on the owner of the worker. The work imposed need not answer to any limitations relating to its conditions or duration or type. The circumstance of being deprived of all formal rights, of being reduced in law to an item of property, is also known as 'chattel' slavery. This was the form of enslavement characteristically imposed upon Africans by Europeans in the transatlantic slaving that began in the fifteenth century. At the extreme, the chattel slave can be bought and sold, removed from the land, from husband or wife, from parent or child. He or she can be made to work in the house or in the fields, in company or isolation, to produce goods or provide services, including sexual services. The chattel can be punished in such degree as the master wishes, up to and including death. Whatever the chattel produces (including offspring) is the property of his or her master, since this slave, in law, has neither title to possessions nor rightful access to dependents or relations. Historically, chattel slavery is met with only rarely. As one writer has observed: 'There has seldom been in history ... any slave-holding community in which the theoretical slave – that is, a thing totally devoid of legal personality and without possessions of his own – has really existed in the actual practice of that community. Only in the confinement of prisons can men be totally deprived of all their freedoms, and hence totally enslaved.'[2]

Fig.25
A slave market in Zabid, Yemen, 1237
Slaves were bought and sold in the markets of the Middle East for centuries.

Chattel slavery, however, is more frequently encountered in large-scale states and empires than in smaller entities. It also assumes its most extreme forms, paradoxically, under the most technologically advanced systems. In brief, chattel slavery, if at first rare, became the slavery of choice for modernity and it was unquestionably harsher, more encompassing and more destructive than ever it proved in antiquity. Europe, in the modern era – from 1492 – opened with, built upon, and persisted in imposing this form of subjection upon Native Americans and Africans for upwards of 400 years. The harshness of transatlantic slavery went hand in hand with the racist sentiments that came to legitimate this traffic. To treat a people with systematic inhumanity depends upon a capacity to break psychic contact with them as fellow humans. Modern slavery was most extreme, precisely because it was comprehensively racist.[3]

How old is slavery?
Slavery, in its comprehensive forms, may be as old as the earliest of states. Evidence for humans 'owning' one another is apparent from Egyptian tomb inscriptions dating back 5,000 years. It is recorded in the poet Homer, writing in the eighth century BC. It is not less prevalent in the Old Testament texts. Yet the type, scale and intensity of slavery is not historically uniform: it waxes and wanes over time. What is clear, however, is the close historical association between the expansion of empire and war, and the extension and worsening of slavery. Early states not only engaged in war for sport, but equally and more importantly, to secure territory, subjects and slaves. Chattel slavery is rare – if we take account of the last 6–10,000 years of human history – but it is not new. The chattel slavery of ancient Greece differed from that of ancient Rome. This differed in turn from that of nineteenth-century Jamaica and Mississippi. Within the Americas, chattel slavery varied from one island or territory or state to the next. Even on the same plantation, the difference in conditions between, for example, the life of 'field slaves' and 'house slaves' could be profound.

There are two constants nonetheless to be remarked. First, the chattel slavery of the Americas was more oppressive than that of ancient Rome, and this more oppressive than that of ancient Greece. Second, the chattel slavery of the American hemisphere absorbed absolutely larger numbers of victims than did Rome, and Rome more than Greece. So chattel slavery, up to little more than a

century ago, was both more extensive and oppressive, in the absolute numbers affected, than ever it was in earlier times. This must raise a large question mark over the character of modernity as a preponderantly progressive era.

What was transatlantic slaving?
This was chattel slavery in its most modern, and almost certainly its worst form. It was begun in the fifteenth century, and ended only in the second half of the nineteenth century – in some cases still later. Even when transatlantic slaving was outlawed, slavery in the Americas continued as before. Even when transatlantic slaving was ended legally, the traffic continued illegally. The conditions of the Atlantic passage were made still worse, in view of the smaller, faster ships, and the closer confinement of victims that they produced. The threat to life was much increased, since ships at risk of being seized would throw their African contraband into the sea to destroy the evidence of their law-breaking.

In the Americas, Columbus took the first Amerindian captives. The effect cumulatively upon native Americans was devastating. In the Caribbean, Amerindians were soon displaced by African captives. The traffic became so enveloping and profitable that the literature still tends to refer to this massacre of the innocents as a trade – 'the African slave trade'. The victims were taken from their native continent on European vessels, transported to the Americas, compelled to work in mines, on farms, the product being exported in turn to Europe.

Did slavery exist in West Africa prior to the arrival of Europeans?
Slavery probably existed in some form in all pre-industrial systems. Certainly it was exploited under all early industrial systems, as in the colonial appendages of Holland, England and France, where chattel slavery was the rule. The question, then, is not, broadly, whether there was slavery in West Africa, but specifically whether a system of chattel slavery was to be found there.

The short answer is 'no'. This answer may be given without qualification for the fifteenth century, but not after we enter the nineteenth century. Slavery was first introduced by force from European vessels upon the tiny village states of the West African forest zone. These states had, and could have, no sense of a common African identity – no more than did Europeans among themselves. The Africans had petty wars among themselves, which normally did not last long, nor do great damage, simply because there were not the surpluses or resources to fuel them. They did not raid one another for slaves because their semi-subsistence economies were not yet elaborate enough to absorb and discipline such labour. The original, small states of the West African forest zone had no capacity to sustain chattel slavery. Thanks to the tsetse fly infestation, they were not subject to significant horse-borne attack from the savannah empires to their north. Nor, before the fifteenth century, had they been vulnerable to attack from the Atlantic. Rulers in this setting had rather few subjects, controlled tiny areas, and were much given to consultation, especially among elders. They could not commonly afford anything quite so grand as 'war', nor be well placed to maintain many individuals, let alone entire populations, as chattels. The Europeans, who came to this coast in ships, were in a position of significant military strength vis-à-vis the Africans whom they encountered, an advantage they compulsively exploited. We simply do not know when slaving began across the Sahara or in East Africa. We do know that there is no evidence for the claim that it existed 'from time immemorial'. As for the Atlantic coast of West Africa, the direct evidence supplied by the Portuguese is that they began the slaving there, not by buying captives, but by kidnapping victims, and by mounting and then sponsoring wars.

Some apologists for European slaving, as Professor Vincent Thompson has archly observed, have been disposed to give 'the impression that (West) Africans themselves started the slave trade, encouraged it, and refused to put an end to it when a benevolent and humanitarian Europe decided that it was time to call a halt'.[4] It makes rather more sense to assume that considerable psychic distance is required for one group to be able to visit upon another such extreme forms of inhumane treatment. The evolving behaviour of the Portuguese towards, for example, the kingdom of the Kongo (contemporary Angola), from the fifteenth into the sixteenth centuries, from a rough egalitarianism into an utterly destructive exploitativeness, is perfectly consistent with the emergence of such psychic distance. Inhumane behaviour, like that of German Nazis towards Jews and Gypsies (1933–1945), will serve as a reliable marker for extreme racist or ethnocentric attitudes and premises. Similar attitudes would appear to have been essential to justify the reduction of Kongolese and other Africans to the status of chattels for sale in Europe and in the Americas. The Portuguese were followed in their slaving and fomenting of war in West Africa by many other European nations. John Hawkins, Francis Drake, Walter Raleigh were all slavers, and given to piracy — enslaving Africans and robbing Spaniards. Hawkins, as late as 1562–63, tells of leading 200 of his men ashore in West Africa – with still drummer, and muffled oar, a strict silence enjoined upon all. This was done in the 'hope that they might surprise a village that Hawkins believed to exist some miles up-country, and capture the inhabitants at daybreak before they had risen from sleep'. Hawkins, like others before and after, learned a more efficient way of pursuing his business. This consisted in locating two small states either at or on the verge of a fight, and throwing his powder and shot to the side of one, thus ensuring victory for his allies and virtually all male captives for himself. These captives were forcibly transported into what for them was a 'New World', and their sale produced for Hawkins a considerable fortune.[5] The Portuguese and other Europeans entered into African slaving determinedly only after their discovery and conquest of the Americas supplied a profitable reason for doing so. Many coastal African statelets sought to escape harm, and to enhance their strength, by entering into alliances with the men from the ships. The balance of power shifted away, quite suddenly, from those societies without, to those with, the backing of European arms. Virtually all West African states thus came directly or indirectly under the tutelage of a shifting succession of European nations. The Europeans, starting with the Portuguese, built their forts and castles in impregnable positions – impregnable at least to attack by land. Africans loyal to them could shelter under the walls of these structures. These Africans could aid the Europeans by supplying slaves, or themselves fall victim to the traffic. Over time, larger and more independent West African states evolved, such as Asante, Dahomey, Oyo and Benin. If they had direct access to the sea, as had Benin, then a firm European dependency was imperative, as in Benin's alliance with the Portuguese. If there was no direct European dependency, then the state – like Asante – would materialize deeper within the forest zone, or even (like Oyo) to the north of the forest, and so more immune to attack from seaward. West African coastal states had little choice but to side with, even while victimized by, European slavers. Over the decades and centuries, Africans were pulled more and more deeply into administering a system of kidnapping, raids and war which proved systematically destructive of their societies. The early states along the

Fig.26
A slave market in Algiers, Dutch engraving, 1684
Africans were also traded across the Sahara and were sold throughout North Africa.

coast, including the very largest and most flourishing of them – Kongo – were torn apart by the 'trade'. Attempts by African rulers to reject, and later to temper, this slaving were consistently repudiated by the European powers in place. This was true very early in the history of African enslavement, as in the case of King Afonso of the Kongo in the sixteenth century,[6] and very late, as in the case of King Troudo of Dahomey in the eighteenth century.[7]

Conclusion

Slavery, generally, emerged hand in hand with government itself. At a time when machinery was rudimentary, human labour was invaluable. War bred slavery. And the value of slaves fomented war. The resources of early states, however, were too paltry to permit practices even vaguely approximating to unlimited war. The division of labour in such entities being so little advanced, the absorption of only the smallest numbers of slaves was feasible. There were not sufficient tasks to give slaves, nor sufficient resources and technology to repress them. Early slavery was systematically more benign, involved more females

18
Anklet
Ivory, West Africa, (?) 18th century

13
Ceremonial sword
Asante, Ghana 19th century

than males, and was overwhelmingly domestic in character. With technological advance, up to and including early industrialization in our own era, slavery became more pathological and regimented, more impersonal and repressive, more global and culturally imperious. Under the chattel regimes of the modern era, the gender selection and racial indifference of the ancient world were reversed. Thus, male victims were markedly more numerous than female. And victims were overwhelmingly more commonly selected by race than by condition or class or national origin. Those who were most distinct in appearance – Africans, then Indians – were those who became most comprehensively victimized. Transatlantic chattel slavery was imposed by Europeans upon the Africans of the Atlantic coast from the fifteenth century. It was sustained for over 400 years, until replaced by systems of colonial tutelage, which themselves commonly resorted to forced African labour. The termination of transatlantic slaving did not terminate slaving as such. For, first, the traffic simply became clandestine. Secondly, the system of slavery itself was not affected, being deeply rooted on both sides of the Atlantic by the nineteenth century. Thirdly, when the system of slavery was itself abolished, various measures were introduced to maintain the state of dependency of the new freedmen, including the introduction into the Americas and elsewhere of bondsmen or indentured labourers from Asia.[8]

Notes

1. In 1572, an act was passed 'for the punishment of Vagabonds and for the Relief of the Poor and Impotent'. It provided for all 'convicted vagabonds above the age of 14 to be whipped and burned through the right ear unless some honest person takes them into service'. An able-bodied person who had no land or money, and was located in or about any large town, was under severe compulsion to submit to a master of some kind. See, for example, A. L. Beir, *The Problem of the Poor in Tudor and Early Stuart England*, London, Methuen, 1983, pp. 34 and 40.

2. See W. L. Westermann, 'Slavery and the Elements of Freedom in Ancient Greece', in M. I. Finlay (ed.), *Slavery in Classical Antiquity*, Cambridge, W. Heffer & Sons, 1960, p. 18.

3. Some of the many books which touch on this question are Thomas Gossett, *Race: The History of an Idea in America*, New York, Schocken Books, 1965; W. Jordan, *White over Black*, Chapel Hill, University of North Carolina Press, 1968; and Joel Kovel, *White Racism: A Psychohistory*, New York, Pantheon, 1970.

4. V. B. Thompson, *The Making of the African Diaspora in the Americas: 1441–1900*, London, Longman, 1987, p. 70. See also B. Davidson, *Old Africa Rediscovered*, London, Victor Gollancz, 1961, pp. 119–20; W. Rodney, *A History of the Upper Guinea Coast, 1545–1880*, Oxford, Clarendon Press, 1970, pp. 40, 260–63 and J. Pope Hennessy, *Sins of the Fathers*, London 1970, p. 182.

5. R. Unwin, *The Defeat of John Hawkins*, London, Penguin, 1962, p. 71f.

6. See J. Duffy, *Portugal in Africa*, London, Penguin, 1962.

7. See John Atkins, *A Voyage to Guinea, Brazil and the West Indies*, London 1737 (2nd edition, reprinted, Frank Cass).

8. See, for example, Hugh Tinker, *A New System of Slavery: The Export of Indian Labour Overseas, 1830–1920*, Oxford, Oxford University Press/Institute of Race Relations, 1977.

The General Legacy
of the Atlantic Slave Trade

STEPHEN SMALL

For the last 500 years the countries of the West have relentlessly exploited Africa and African people. Millions of Africans were murdered, millions more violently kidnapped and enslaved, women raped and brutalized, and African societies totally ransacked. Slavery and colonialism were carried out for the economic enrichment of the West, with the full legal and political sanction of presidents, prime ministers and the Church. It was exploitation of African labour that led to the expansion of industry across Britain, the United States and the world. At the same time, slavery and colonialism created the circumstances which confine Africans and African nations to the worst conditions experienced by any people in the world today. In the light of these facts, where does one begin to evaluate the effects of the Atlantic slave trade in a world in which, almost 190 years after the slave trade was abolished across the British Empire, and over 150 years after slavery was abolished, Africans and the descendants of Africans remain at such a dire institutional disadvantage compared to those who promoted the trade against them? The millions now starving in Africa can trace their plight to slavery and colonialism, and the poverty they experience is worse than in any other area of the globe. Raw materials and natural assets are ravaged from their rightful owners under shallow promises of fair trading and tawdry policies of arms for aid. Political instability continues to plague territories established around the arbitrary and self-serving boundaries imposed by Europeans. Military dictatorships are responsible for some of the desperation that confronts the continent's millions, but even these have often been set up and supported by duplicitous governments of the West.

In South America and the Caribbean, economies remain underdeveloped and stagnant, people occupy shanty-town dwellings and there is inadequate provision for the educational and health needs of children. Transnational companies exploit cheap labour and lax environmental regulation, even using vulnerable populations to offload tobacco and alcohol, and to dispose of chemical and industrial waste. In those areas exploited and abandoned by the nations which profited from the Atlantic slave trade, economies continue to find that the World Bank, under the total control of Europeans and Americans, is a more powerful dictate of their essential policies than any indigenous head of state. In the United States and across Europe the descendants of Africans struggle to survive violent attacks, systematic racial hostility, and the continued vilification of Africans and 'blackness'. Formal immigration legislation and institutional practices across 'fortress Europe' are designed to keep Africans out; racial hostility constrains their movements within. It is little wonder that Africans and their descendants live a quality of life fundamentally different from that of Europeans and their descendants. No wonder then that Dubois, one of the most unrelenting advocates of equality for Africa and Africans, could predict in 1903: 'The problem of the twentieth century is the problem of the colour line – the relation of the darker to the lighter races of men in Asia and Africa, in America and in the islands of the sea.'

Evaluating the legacy of slavery

There are few who would doubt that slavery has contributed in fundamental ways to the shape of the contemporary world, and to relations between Africa, the Americas and Europe. But having identified some of the links between slavery and current racial inequality, the difficult question is to establish exactly how it contributed. More specifically, to establish patterns and relationships of causality. An evaluation of the legacy of slavery must take as its starting point the present circumstances within which the descendants of slaves, and of slave masters and their families, find themselves. But there is often divergence around this evaluation. Some analysts claim we cannot understand racial inequality in the 1990s without fundamentally appreciating the legacy of slavery in all its effects. For this group, poverty and powerlessness in Africa, South America and the Caribbean, and racial inequality for black people in the west, is a direct consequence of the Atlantic slave trade, and of the colonial system to which it gave rise. But there are others who say that the causes of current racial inequality, and the factors that perpetuate it, can only be understood in terms of current conditions, current power relations and current conflict. These analysts point to the failed economic and social policies of territories once dominated by Europeans, and to inflexible economies and political dictators. No one has yet established the criteria by which we might establish which is the right or best answer. Not least because the legacy of slavery is still unfolding and new developments affect our evaluation.

In any case, it would be premature at this stage to decide exactly what the full effects have been, or how best to measure them. Their influence continues, and it is far too early for a definitive evaluation of this pestilence of history. At the moment it seem wisest to accept that both past and present conditions have contributed in myriad ways, and recognize that the precise influence of each of them is likely to remain beyond our full explanation.

If we are to begin to assess the legacy of the Atlantic slave trade, then we must first appreciate that the collective memory of slavery of Africans and their descendants is vastly different from that of Europeans and their descendants. To most white people, slavery and colonialism are just a distant memory of nothing in particular. For whites, slavery did not last particularly long, its benefits accrued only to a tiny proportion of white people and the evils of slavery are overshadowed by the role played by British abolitionists. In any case, the rise of Western nations, Britain and the United States in particular, as the industrial supremos of the world, is explicable to them simply in terms of English innate genius. Poverty and penury in Africa, and racial inequality in the West, is explained in terms of black inability, incompetence or laziness.

To black people, though, slavery and colonialism reiterate themselves in our everyday lives, and evoke poignant and immediate memories of suffering, brutalization and terror. For black people, Western nations achieved their industrial growth and economic prosperity on the backs of blacks, abolished slavery primarily for economic reasons, have discriminated against black people ever since, and are unrepentant about any of it. African underdevelopment and racial inequality in the West is understood primarily in terms of racism and the racist hostility of whites. It is these divergent interpretations of the effects of slavery that resulted in so many whites and so few blacks in 1992 celebrating Columbus.

But surely we must conclude that the legacy is not all negative? There are some who focus on the cultural benefits that have arisen from the crossing of cultures to which slavery gave rise – of music, dance, art and cuisine. Certainly such benefits must be celebrated, but only in the context of the continued degradation of Africa and Africans. For every person who celebrated 500 years of Columbus, there is another who curses Columbus, celebrates 500 years of resistance, and urges more.

Aspects of the legacy

The enslavement of Africans and the growth and proliferation of European racisms is inextricably intertwined both with the systems of economic, political and social relations which immediately followed its abolition and with the current contours of the international economic, political and social system, and the gross extremes of inequality which characterize it. There were variations from place to place, but many continuities remained. The legacy of slavery is reiterated in the following.

Economic systems and population movements

As advanced industrial capitalist societies based on wage labour and liberal democracy, countries such as Britain, the United States, France, Spain, Portugal and the Netherlands have all achieved substantial economic development via conquest, slavery and the exploitation of African labour. It was this labour that fed financial accumulation, economic expansion and the base for industrial acquisition, that is, the development of capitalism.

Central to the international economic system which we now share have been the mass migrations that populated (and depopulated) the Americas – migrations which have led to the Diasporic presence throughout Europe and the Americas.

195
Banshee, the first of the 'blockade runners' built in Liverpool for the Confederate states in the US Civil War
Builders' model, 1863

Racialization and racist ideologies

'Racialization' simply means the process by which Africans and Europeans came to be defined as races. This is a historical process born of the contact between the two continents, of the goals of Europeans and of the unequal power relations between the two. It is during slavery and colonialism that racist ideologies were developed and disseminated. The end of slavery saw racist ideologies reshaped to meet the complex and changing conditions of industrialization, but with a brutal consistency in their vilification of Africans and insistence of black inferiority.

Racist theories continued to be developed by the most distinguished and respected scientists of Europe and North America, who seized upon science to 'justify' oppression, exploitation and injustice. In the contemporary world, evidence abounds of multiple 'racisms' as the rationalizations used to assert African inferiority have been rearticulated, advocacy of racial hostility has moved from the overt to the covert, and racism has become, in the words of Sivanandan, 'less visible but no less virulent'.

Racist ideologies underlie the enduring effects of racial group barriers, boundaries and identities in the modern world. These ideologies have continued to plague blacks throughout the continent and the Diaspora. There are at least two reasons for this. One is that such ideologies were deliberately modified by whites in the light of post-slavery circumstances. A second reason is that racial identities and antipathies established during slavery set in process institutional practices which continued after slavery ended – for example, those around colour, where conflict has continued at various levels between those of different shades in the black community.

Institutional racist practices

From the *de facto* subordination of Africans across European colonies and apartheid in South Africa, to legal segregation in the United States and discrimination across Europe, institutional racist practices have been central to the creation of modern nation states (both inside and outside Europe) and current conflicts in Africa, South America and the Caribbean. Racist practices also shaped the realities of citizenship and non-citizenship, and the extension or denial of the inalienable right to life, liberty and the pursuit of happiness.

In those nations that promoted slavery, white exclusionary practices continued to operate after its demise – based on notions of biological inferiority here, cultural inferiority there – and systematic racial discrimination has led to the concentration of blacks in the most disadvantaged sections of society. Even now, many whites hold racist views about who qualifies as a full member of the country and community, views which have often become enshrined in institutional form, particularly in immigration legislation. Western nations have thus struggled with the ideals that they espouse and have failed to extend those ideals to Africans and other minorities. So despite lofty ideals of freedom, equality, democracy and fairness, these countries have systematically excluded Africans and their descendants from the benefits of such ideals.

The duplicity of Western governments

Successive governments during and since slavery have continued to play a role in rearticulating racial ideology and in managing the racial crisis, often engaging in conflicting and contradictory methods – denial here, compromise there, defeat elsewhere. Governments have been the prime movers of racist ideologies and practices under apartheid in South Africa, through forced colonial labour across African colonies dominated by the West, through the Supreme Court in the United States and through immigration legislation in Britain and France.

Currently, these governments share a focus on the use of anti-discrimination laws as mechanisms for defusing social conflict and breaking down patterns of disadvantage and discrimination. While relatively strong on paper, such laws have often been limited in practical effect, and the integrity of governments is challenged by the fact that much of their immigration legislation is predicated on racist assumptions. The current attempts to consolidate a 'fortress Europe', white on the inside, Africans and people of colour excluded, or marginalized within, perpetuate the impact of racial hostility.

The colour line

The overarching similarity across these nations, with modifications, is of course the 'colour line' – the inequality between white and black of wealth, income, employment, education, health and housing – which characterizes the African experience. Wealth, affluence and good health are enjoyed overwhelmingly by the majority of the world's population, which is white; while poverty and ill health befall Africans and their descendants.

Communities of resistance

The legacy of slavery has everywhere given rise to sustained response by people of African origin, and to cultures and communities of resistance. Continued injustice and exclusion gave rise to separate, and separatist, groups, organizations and institutions based on notions of autonomy and self-determination for black people, from national and international movements such as black

nationalism, Pan-Africanism and Negritude, to black organizations and groups, black individuals and a whole array of nationalist and anti-imperialist movements across the length and breadth of Africa.

For example, in Africa, from Kwame Nkrumah, Jomo Kenyatta and Julius Nyerere to Robert Mugabe, Nelson Mandela and Leopold Senghor. In the Caribbean, from Paul Bogle and George William Gordon to Franz Fanon and Marcus Garvey; from Michael Manley and Maurice Bishop to C.L.R. James. In the United States, from the Negro Academy and the National Association of Colored Women to the Urban League, the Nation of Islam, the Southern Christian Leadership Conference and the Black Panther Party. From Sojourner Truth and Ida B. Wells to Mary Mcloud Bethune and Mary Church Terrell, and from Rosa Parks to Angela Davis. In Britain, the League of Coloured Peoples, the Campaign Against Racial Discrimination, the West Indian Standing Conference, the Race Today Collective and the Institute of Race Relations. In France, the activities of Leopold Senghor and Aimé Cesaire and Léon-Gotran Dumas. Cultures and communities of resistance have always been international, as links across the Diaspora were established and sustained. Black people have always looked across the Diaspora – and travelled across it – for comfort, support and ideas. Africans, African Americans and African Caribbeans actively travelled to challenge slavery, colonialism and imperialism, and were foremost in the successful national liberation struggles. These advocates of equality and self-determination visited numerous countries to establish the Pan-African Congress, whose meetings were attended by the soon-to-be leaders of African nations – Kwame Nkrumah, Jomo Kenyatta and Julius Nyerere.

Black people in England have also looked abroad for inspiration and encouragement; from Olaudah Equiano and Ottobah Cuguano to Ignatius Sancho – names which should roll off our tongues easily but do not because we are not told about them at school – who played decisive roles in the campaign to abolish the slave trade and slavery. They went beyond our differences to demand and defend the interests of the black community as a whole.

A central concern in such struggles has been the idea, ideal and reality of Africa, as concept and inspiration, perhaps summed up best in Garvey's argument in favour of 'Africa for the Africans, at home and abroad'. One part of Garvey's great mission was to return Diasporic Africans to the continent, but a greater and larger mission was to make Africa a place to which Africans throughout the Diaspora could look with pride and self-respect when oppressed or exploited for being African.

While the efforts of those who were most successful are bound to attract our attention, we must also and always recognize the efforts of those many thousands who struggled without reward, without credit, without fame or fortune, but without whom great leaders would never become great, and without whom not even 1 per cent of what has been achieved would ever have been achieved.

Resistance remains central in the efforts of people of African origin – and their allies – to come together to contain the worst atrocities of racial injustice, and to establish agendas, priorities, political action and policies to overcome them. Its most current articulation around slavery is reflected in the reparations movement.

Reparations

During the 1990s black people began demanding reparations from the nations of the West for the atrocities, injustice and exploitation perpetrated against Africa and Africans during slavery and colonialism. An international conference took place in Abuja, Nigeria, in April 1993, attended by representatives of the Organisation of African Unity, members of African national governments, and distinguished scholars and lawyers. The Abuja Conference was attended by Bernie Grant, MP for Tottenham, London, who put forward a motion in the House of Commons demanding that the issue of reparations be debated.

In Britain a steering committee was established to co-ordinate activities: Reparations U.K. It demands that Europe and the United States acknowledge the crimes committed during slavery and the benefits they have enjoyed, and pay for what they have done via reparations. Reparations is a legally enforced repayment for the damage and destruction caused. Reparations were made by the German government to Israel for the Jewish victims of the Nazi Holocaust; reparations were made by the United States' government to the Japanese and Japanese Americans interned during World War Two. In other words, a clear legal precedent has been established.

The Reparations movement believes that Europe and the United States must cancel financial debts, or transfer capital, or offer services to those they have victimized, or find some other way of making restitution. They must also return the treasures stolen from African societies, and currently housed in the museums of the West. As a matter of urgency, they must meet with the heads of African nations, and with representatives of African peoples elsewhere, to decide how this can be done.

The Reparations movement believes that its case is morally right, economically sound, politically inevitable, and legally inescapable. But it must convince those who wield the power and economic benefits derived from slavery of the rightness of their case. The Reparations movement believes that all who are committed to justice, and to ensuring that the whole of the world's population benefits from the hard work of past and present generations, must support black people's demands for reparations.

Conclusion

The effects of the Atlantic slave trade are palpable across the world today; they are most prominent in the minds of Africans and their descendants. The particular impact the Atlantic slave trade has had varies from continent to continent, from country to country and within countries. But the consequences of the devastation it caused remain. This makes the European trade in Africans more significant, and its impact more immediate, than any other system of slavery. The question of whether slavery alone caused the present conditions across Africa, or the Americas, or Europe, becomes irrelevant. The key issue is that current contours of racial injustice, hostility and inequality can be traced directly to the Atlantic slave trade, and the memory of slavery remains prominent in the minds of Africa and her children.

The descendants of Africans and of Europeans view the legacy of the slave trade from different vantage points. This is bound to be the case in the immediate future, and we can expect no consensus. Without acknowledgement and action, it could remain the case indefinitely. Africans and Europeans recognize that the changes brought about by the Atlantic slave trade are irreversible. Africans and their descendants realize that there is nothing that the West can ever do to make right the wrongs committed during slavery and colonialism. But they also insist that the West can begin to loosen the shackles of poverty and economic distress which continue to hold back Africans and Africa. It is these obstacles enshrined in the international, economic and political infrastructure of trade, more than anything, which impede the development of Africa and the rights of Africans' descendants. Only by tackling the unfairness of these systems can we begin together to create a more morally acceptable economic and political system within which the world's entire population can prosper.

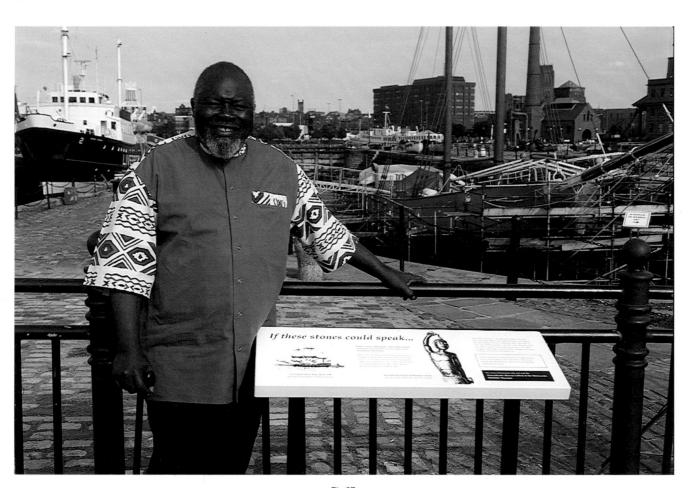

Fig.27
Bernie Grant, MP, at the Merseyside Maritime Museum quayside on Slavery Remembrance Day, 1999

The Challenge
of Remembering Slavery

LONNIE G. BUNCH

'The Challenge of Remembering Slavery' was presented at the Merseyside Maritime Museum as the first International Slavery Day Lecture in August 2003. NML has championed UNESCO's International Day for the Remembrance of the Slave Trade and its Abolition on 23 August each year since 1999. Lonnie G. Bunch is Director of the National Museum of African American History and Culture, Washington DC.

Thank you for the warm introduction and welcome. I am honoured to be a part of the Slavery Remembrance Day activities. And I am humbled by the fact that such an event as this has not taken place in the U.S. I applaud the National Museums Liverpool for their leadership in working to make this an annual, global event. I want to express my gratitude to Dr David Fleming and to Garry Morris for their kind invitation. I want to acknowledge the efforts of Garry Morris who has worked so hard to create this programme.

Early in my career I crafted an exhibition at the Smithsonian Institution's National Museum of American History that was to explore the role and history of American slavery. I travelled throughout the American South searching for an extant slave cabin that I could use in the exhibition. Ultimately, I found a cabin on the old Friendfield Plantation that was located in the rice-producing area of the Wacamaw Neck near Georgetown, South Carolina. After driving past an array of swamps, I came to a 'slave street', an area that contained twelve slave cabins and a small church. There I met Mr Johnson. Mr Johnson was the grandson of a slave who had resided in one of these cabins from the 1850s until her death in the 1930s. Mr Johnson was a wonderful source who told me many stories about the way slaves used their cabins. As we walked to the front of the cabin, Mr Johnson talked about how the slaves did a 'hard sweep' that

eliminated the grass and weeds that were the home to vermin. And then we walked to the side where the chimney was located and he spoke about the role that slave children played in maintaining the chimneys to prevent fires. And then we moved to the rear of the cabin where he explained how slaves used that space to grow food crops that supplemented the food that was provided by the owners. Finally, I walked to the fourth side but Mr Johnson did not follow me. After repeatedly asking him to accompany me, I demanded to know why he left me alone on that side of the cabin. Finally he looked at me and said that he would not move in my direction because the area 'was full of poisonous snakes!' After I stopped running, I asked why he did not warn me. He said that everyone around here knows the history of that spot. And then he said, 'people need to remember about slavery. It pains the ancestors when we forget.' His words – 'people need to remember' – have never left me. I am haunted by Mr Johnson's call to remember. Haunted because in America, there is not a day or even a moment set aside to remember publicly our slave past. I am haunted by the fact that not knowing and not remembering the history, legacy and contemporary meaning of slavery hurts the living and dishonours the millions who experienced the slave trade; survived the institution of slavery; or who fought for the abolition of this great evil.

125

In a way, events like Slavery Remembrance Day are an appropriate and fitting tribute to our ancestors, because it gives voice to the anonymous and makes the unseen visible. And because a day such as this ensures that the people will remember. But it is essential that our remembering transcends a passive nostalgia that simply acknowledges this history. Rather we must find the contemporary resonance. We must find a past that is useful and meaningful to living generations. In the words of James Baldwin, the gifted African American novelist from his work, *The Fire Next Time*, we must realize 'that history does not refer merely or even principally to the past. On the contrary, the great face of history comes from the fact that we carry it within us, we are unconsciously controlled by it in many ways, and the history is literally present in all that we do'. Or as the nineteenth-century philosopher once wrote, 'unless we deal with the rough and smooth edges of a country's past, the experiences of earlier generations weighs like a nightmare on the brain of the living'.

Clearly we are all touched and shaped by the experience of slavery, and yet, how do we find this useful and useable past? And what are some of the challenges that stand in the way of honouring our ancestors? Let me briefly lay out some of these challenges and offer some suggestions as to how we can ensure that we can honour our ancestors.

Grappling with a country's tendency to forget
I would suggest that you can tell a great deal about a country or a people by what they deem important enough to remember, what they build monuments to celebrate, what graces their museums, and what holidays they embrace. Throughout Scandinavia, there are monuments and museums that cherish the Vikings as a symbol of identity, exploration and freedom. Until recently, the monuments and the memories of the Voertrekkers dominated South Africa, while America traditionally revels in monuments that celebrate Civil War battles or the founding fathers of the American Revolution – with an occasional politician thrown into the mix.

Yet I would argue that we learn even more about a country from whom and what it chooses to forget, what Nietszche called 'creative forgetfulness'. This desire to edit the past, to omit uncomfortable or embarrassing history, no matter how important, is quite instructive. Yet the history of slavery is too important to simply allow it to be cloaked in silence.

Nowhere is this silence more deafening than in America. For more than 250 years slavery cast a dramatic and costly shadow over the United States. Slavery was one of the dominant institutions in American life. Political clout and economic fortune depended upon the labour of slaves. Almost every aspect of American life from business to religion, from culture to commerce, from foreign policy to western expansion, was informed by the slave experience. The most devastating war in American history – the Civil War – was fought over slavery, yet in 2003 there are surprisingly few opportunities for the general public to engage candidly and openly with the impact, racial legacy and contemporary meaning of slavery.

It was little more than a decade ago that historic sites and museums in America began raising the subject of slavery. Most historic homes and plantations celebrated the elite but rarely mentioned the slave, celebrated the product (cotton or tobacco) but not the people who produced the product. Important plantations like Mount Vernon (home of George Washington) and Monticello (home of Thomas Jefferson) never even used the word slave or enslaved – their tours always mentioned the servants. And when slaves were discussed, it was usually a depiction of the loyal retainer. The best example is the Hermitage – the plantation of Andrew Jackson. There Jackson's personal slave, Alfred, is celebrated, the tourists are pointed to his grave, which is at the feet of Jackson – as if Alfred was to serve Jackson through all of eternity.

In the last decade there have been important changes in America. Some plantations such as Monticello now offer tours of the slave cabins. As an aside, the best of these tours focuses on the Somerset Plantation in North Carolina. And several museums – from the Museum of the Confederacy, to the Smithsonian Institution, to Mariners' Museum, Virginia, to the Library of Congress – have mounted temporary exhibitions that have raised the level of interest in this subject. Yet few American cultural institutions have dedicated the space, expended the intellectual and scholarly capital and made the public commitment to explore slavery in a way that is comprehensive, accessible and willing to grapple with both the historical legacy and contemporary meaning of slavery.

Why? Because surveys and public sentiment suggests that Americans are ambivalent at best, but more often hostile to discussions about slavery. Not too long ago, I interviewed former President Bill Clinton on his administration. When I asked him what was the biggest

126
'The TOBACCO MANUFACTORY in different Branches'
Engraving, laid off-white paper and black ink, 1750

surprise he experienced – no, it is not what you think – he said that he was stunned by the overwhelming and negative response he received when he mentioned the possibility of the President apologizing about slavery. Equally surprising to me was a survey commissioned by the National Museum of American History in 1990. When the Smithsonian decided to mount an exhibition on slavery, the central administration demanded a survey to find out what Americans knew and thought about slavery. The results were fascinating and troubling. And yet they also provided insight on America's reluctance to explore slavery.

Of the white respondents, 84% felt that slavery had little or no direct meaning for them. And 80% of whites felt that slavery was simply an African American story. And

even more fascinating was the fact that 79% of black Americans expressed either no interest or great embarrassment about slavery. And 61% of blacks suggested that the Smithsonian would be better served putting its resources elsewhere.

I share these numbers, not to suggest how hopeless America is, but to reinforce why an International Day of Remembrance is so important. Much of this ambivalence comes from ignorance and a lack of understanding about slavery. If we are to honour our ancestors, in America, it is important that we dramatically shift the paradigm that defines our notions about the lives of the men and women who were enslaved.

Shifting the paradigm

In 1937 a former slave, William Prescott, was interviewed about his life as a slave. Prescott was one of hundreds of elderly freed men and women who were interviewed by out-of-work historians hired by the American government during the Great Depression. Prescott had spent his whole life on the rice plantation that he worked as a slave. When asked about his long life, he wondered what future generations would think about the enslaved. He said, 'it is something but soon there won't be anyone alive who was a slave'. Prescott went on to say that he was saddened because 'they will remember that we were sold but they won't remember that we were strong. They will remember that we were bought, but not that we were brave.'

It is sad, but William Prescott was correct. Many people – especially, but not solely, Americans – are embarrassed by their slave past. For many, the word 'slave' conjures up negative images of backbreaking labour, the separation of families, people bent by fear and violence, and a sense of racial inferiority. These images generate thoughts of anger, shame, loss and discomfort. So much discomfort that I once received a letter from a leading politician who wrote, 'Just make slavery go away'. The importance of Slavery Remembrance Day is to ensure that the memory and the meaning of slavery never disappear. Rather than feel ashamed, I hope that people will celebrate, explore and remember. I hope that the sense of shame will be replaced by other emotions. Personally, I am in awe of our slave ancestors. I wish we all had their strength, their resiliency, and their creativity, their optimism, and their belief that change was inevitable.

I stand in awe of the will that enabled millions to survive the 'middle passage'. I am moved by the courage of those who struck blows against the institution of slavery – and by those who ran away to freedom. I am humbled by the actions of Harriet Tubman, Frederick Douglass, and Toussaint L'Ouverture. But I am even more impressed by the nameless men and women who arose each day and vowed that the field would not break them; or by those who despite the workload struggled to ensure that there would be energy left for the family; or those who struggled to keep their culture alive, their humour and their humanity intact. In essence, it is crucial that we remember, because these ancestors are the best role models one can every find.

Rather than shame, we should find strength; rather than hopelessness, we should find hope; rather than loss, we should find ourselves. And rather than forget, we should remember.

139
Slave badge, stamped 'CHARLESTON / 1392 / SERVANT / 1846
Copper alloy, 1846

But remembering is not enough. From these memories we should also draw sustenance, inspiration, and relevancy for the struggles for social justice that are so part of our world today. What better models for achievement against the odds are there than those enslaved men and women? I am particularly touched by the efforts of thousands – men and women, black and white, American and English, the religious and the secular, free and slave – who participated in a struggle that seemed overwhelming – the struggle to abolish slavery. From the vantage point of the turn of the nineteenth century, few would have believed that an institution that fuelled the industrial revolution, a system that was the backbone of the American economy, and a means of social control that determined and altered racial relations globally, could be attacked successfully – from outside and from within – by such a diverse and shifting array of individuals and organizations. The struggle to end slavery was one of humanity's great achievements: one that should help us all realize that profound change is possible. It is not without loss, it is not without sacrifice, it is not without coalitions, and it is not without faith and patience. I am not sure that we realize just how remarkable abolition was.

Let me share one story about the inspirational connection between the historic efforts to end slavery and a more contemporary struggle for social justice. In 1997, I

Fig.28
Blue glass rolling pin with abolitionist verse
Sunderland, c.1820–40

was lecturing in South Africa when I found myself in the small city of Pietermaritzburg, which is located in Durban in Kwa Zulu Natal. This city has a significant Indian population and it was the site of Mahatma Gandhi's first brush with the racism of South Africa in 1903. While I was there, Nelson Mandela came to this city that was the ancestral homeland of his political and tribal rivals – the Zulus. He was to receive 'the freedom of the city'. I was privileged to sit on the podium as Mandela gave his speech. As is his custom he spoke in several languages – from Xhosa to Zulu to N'debele – about his struggles against apartheid. And then in English he spoke about his 27 years in the prison on Robben Island. He said that one of the things that gave him strength and substance was the history of the struggle for racial equality in America. He spoke passionately and eloquently of how American abolitionists such as Sojourner Truth, Harriet Tubman, William Lloyd Garrison and Frederick Douglass inspired him and helped him to believe that freedom and racial transformation were possible in South Africa. After his presentation, we talked a bit and he emphasized how that history gave him comfort and a sense of the possible, even during some of his most difficult hours. Finding inspiration from this struggle is an important way to pay tribute to our ancestors in the twenty-first century.

We also pay homage to our ancestors if we use the slave past as a way to stimulate debate and discourse on contemporary racial relations, and if we can reposition slavery within our national discourse. In America, for example, one of the reasons that slavery has not been at the centre of our public memory is because slavery is not seen as a quintessential American story. In the survey that I cited earlier, overwhelmingly white Americans saw slavery as simply a black story that, while important, had little direct impact in their lives or their histories. Thus slavery in America has been marginalized as just something that affected the 13% of the population that is African American. Yet it is crucial that we reposition the argument so that all see that remembering slavery and abolition is not just an African story, but it is also an American story, it is not just monumental for blacks, but it is crucial for all of England, all of Europe. By 're-centring slavery' we can return slavery and race to a position that echoes its centrality and its prominence of earlier centuries.

Ultimately, Slavery Remembrance Day is crucial because it is a wonderful but uncompromising mirror. A mirror that reminds us of our struggles and of our losses. But it is also a mirror that reminds us of noble ideals, of promises kept, and dreams and struggles that come true. Slavery Remembrance Day is a mirror that illuminates the darker corners of our history. It is a mirror that gives visibility and voice to the millions of Africans who are lost to history. Yet this day also reminds us of our commonalities, our shared culture, and our responsibilities to continue to struggle, to fight the good fight for racial and social injustice. But most importantly, Slavery Remembrance Day is a clarion call to remember. And there is no more powerful force than a country or a people steeped in their history. And there is no higher cause than honouring our ancestors and their struggles by remembering.

Let me conclude with a quotation from a former slave, Cornelius Holmes, who said in 1939, 'though the slavery question is settled, its impact is not The question will be with us always. It is in our politics, it is in our courts, and it is on our highways, it is in our manner, in our religion and in our thoughts. All the day – everyday.'

What a great gift to the people of England and to the people of America, if we can ensure that Slavery Remembrance Day can help us all remember that we are touched by slavery – all the day – everyday.

Flagellation of a Female Samboe Slave.

Fig.29
'Flagellation of a female slave' from J. G. Stedman, *Narrative of a five year
expedition against the Revolted Negroes of Surinam, 1772-77,* London 1796

Interpreting Transatlantic Slavery: The Role of Museums

ANTHONY TIBBLES

In the last forty years the growth in the academic study of the transatlantic slave trade and transatlantic slavery has been phenomenal. By contrast, museums in the three continents affected by the Diaspora have been slower to respond. In the last decade there have been some notable developments in terms of both temporary exhibitions and permanent displays. This reflects both a recognition that uncomfortable and controversial issues can and should be explored by museums and also that there is significant public interest in the subject matter. This article traces some of the more important developments in the response of museums in addressing transatlantic slavery and the slave trade, particularly in Britain, Europe and the United States and contrasts the experience. The development of the *Transatlantic Slavery* gallery at the Merseyside Maritime Museum in Liverpool will provide a point of reference. The article also looks at the problems of interpretation of material culture related to transatlantic slavery and offers some thoughts for the future.

It is perhaps not surprising that the main developments have been in museums in Europe and the United States; for a variety of reasons, principally related to the economic situation, museums in Africa, South America and the Caribbean have been unable to mirror this.[1] In Britain, the beginnings of museum interest and activity in this subject can be seen in the development of multiculturalism in the 1980s. Many museums have large ethnographic collections, mainly acquired in the last century as a result of colonial activity, and for many years quite an embarrassment to them. They were unsure in a post-colonial era how they should deal with such material. For many, feeling uncomfortable meant that they did nothing and the

collections either languished in out-of-date displays or were kept out of sight in store rooms. However, in 1986 the City Museum & Art Gallery in Birmingham valiantly took up the challenge with its *Gallery 33* project which was an attempt to re-define its ethnographic collections in the context of a multicultural society.[2] A crucial element of the preparations was dialogue with local ethnic communities about the proposal. Although very limited in scope, this represented a recognition that the local people had a role to play in how their own cultures were displayed and interpreted.

In terms of addressing issues directly related to the black Atlantic, the earliest initiatives in Britain began by looking at the black presence, initially through a number of temporary exhibitions examining the history of local black communities. The first of these exhibitions, in 1991, *Staying Power: the Black presence in Liverpool*, was the result of collaboration between the then Museum of Labour History, part of National Museums & Galleries on Merseyside (NMGM), Liverpool Anti-Racist and Community Arts Association and Liverpool City Council.[3] Another exhibition in 1993 explored the history of the black community in Nottingham.[4]

At about the same time, the Museum of London also realized that its displays spoke almost exclusively to the white population. It began a wide-ranging project, *The Peopling of London*, which resulted in a major exhibition at the museum in 1993–4. This looked at the migration of different peoples and communities over 2,000 years of the city's history and within this included sections on the black presence.[5]

All these exhibitions had to address the question 'How did the black community get here?' and this immediately led to the subject of the transatlantic slave trade. It is clear that transatlantic slavery and the slave trade were subjects almost universally ignored by museums, especially in those cities most closely involved with its prosecution. Indeed, the only permanent display dealing with the slave trade at that time was in Hull – in the former home of William Wilberforce – which has been a museum to his memory since 1906. The collections of anti-slavery material which have been built up over the years are very significant. New displays on the slave trade and its abolition were installed in 1986 but were limited in terms of both the interpretative approach and the execution. Despite the shortcomings it is perhaps still surprising that the impact was so limited.

The wider issue of slavery was partially addressed by a series of temporary exhibitions looking at the legacies of Britain's colonial past held in Bristol, Liverpool and Hull under the title *Trophies of Empire* in 1992. In particularly Keith Piper's video installation, *Trade Winds*, explored the relationship between the slave trade and the development of contemporary global capitalism.[6]

The amnesia of museums in relation to the slave trade and its impact was no more starkly demonstrated than in Liverpool, the port which dominated the slave trade in the eighteenth century. The earliest contributions were meagre: some shackles and little more than a label were included in the Port of Liverpool gallery in the Liverpool Museum, opened in 1975. As late as 1987, the museum failed to provide an adequate presentation on the importance of the slave trade in the Merseyside Maritime Museum's new gallery on the early history of the port. The gallery was based on inadequate research and it rightly drew criticism.[7]

It was not long after this in 1990, when internal discussions had begun on what could be done to improve the gallery and address the criticism, that the Peter Moores Foundation approached National Museums Liverpool (NML) with the suggestion of creating a display about the slave trade.[8] The initiative came from the Foundation's founder and patron, Peter Moores, whose own interest in the subject had been generated by what he saw as a need to come to terms with the past and to face up to the issues raised. After several months of discussion NML came to an agreement whereby the Foundation would make available nearly £550,000 for the development of a 400 sq. metre gallery devoted to the transatlantic slave trade in the basement of the maritime museum.

When in December 1991 the partnership to create the gallery was launched, there was concern and suspicion not only of the Foundation but also of NML. Why was NML doing it? What was the museum getting out of it? Who was doing it? What role did people outside the museum have? Understandably, these questions were most directly asked by people in the black community in Liverpool. There were other pressures such as the Foundation's requirement to be factual and accurate. And there was the admonition from one of the other key players that white people should not leave feeling guilty and that black people should not leave feeling angry. NML set up an internal project team, brought together an international group of academics to act as guest curators, and established an advisory committee drawn from people representative of interests on a local, national and international basis. Consultation was also undertaken with black groups and individuals both locally and more widely.[9]

The result is a gallery which tries to look at the whole history of the transatlantic slave trade, not comprehensively, but in terms of the involvement and the impact, maintaining a local input but not neglecting the international perspective.[10] It attempts to reflect the experience of transatlantic slavery over a 400-year period, between three continents and to tell a human story rather than technical one. After much discussion the gallery opened under the title *Transatlantic Slavery: Against Human Dignity*.

The gallery displays begin with an introduction area explaining the operation of the trade and setting it in context as primarily a human story, about people not statistics. This is followed by a brief section on why Africans were needed as labour in the Americas. The first major section looks at West and Central West Africa before and during slavery, indicating the range of its societies and culture through objects, illustrations, contemporary witness and music. European involvement in Africa and the demands of trading are covered with the centrepiece being a diorama of the trading process in action and a display of typical trade goods. European countries, their merchants, ships and organizations are indicated before the visitor passes into a reconstruction of part of the hold of a slave ship. This is deliberately empty, except for simulated movement of figures on the decks and shelves and the alternating voices of Equiano reading from his *Narrative* and John Newton reading from the log of one his voyages. It is intended to recreate the physical space and to encourage visitors to use their own imaginations.

A more traditional display on conditions on board ship adjoins the reconstruction and then visitors find out where Africans were taken and how they were sold, culminating in a diorama of a slave auction in Brazil. A video based on contemporary accounts of slave life in the Americas follows with supporting objects, illustrations and even some living sugar cane. The profits of slavery for the Europeans are explored through objects, illustrations and a computer interactive program. The last sections look at the struggle for abolition and emancipation and the role of different factors – African resistance, economic factors and the humanitarian campaigns – in bringing the trade and transatlantic slavery to an end. The final display in the gallery is a commissioned video exploring the lives of black people in Britain today and allowing them to voice their views on slavery and its legacy.

One key comment made during the development of the gallery was that NMGM should not see the gallery as a one-off; black people were looking for a long-term commitment. As an immediate response the museum took opportunities to include appropriate elements in its programme – one such was the *Trade Winds* installation by Keith Piper in the *Trophies of Empire* exhibitions mentioned above. The appointment of an outreach worker was made in 1993 and he initially organized workshops and activities in the six months leading up to the opening.

The gallery was officially opened by Maya Angelou in October 1994. An inter-denominational service was held at the Cathedral, a street procession and performance based on the infamous *Zong* incident were held and an African libation was incorporated in the opening ceremony. A series of supporting exhibitions and displays and lectures together with other activities were held, and associated educational resources and programmes developed.

The gallery touched a nerve. The public response was tremendous, drawing double the usual number of visitors for its first few weeks and sustaining that interest at about 30% above normally for the following six months. It has continued to be a significant draw and it is still the most visited gallery in the museum, with almost a third of all visitors making it their first choice on entering the museum. Evaluation has shown that people learn and are stimulated by the gallery and its subject matter to a much higher level than is the case with museum visiting in general.

In the ten years since the gallery opened, NML has continued to maintain a range of public and educational activities associated with the gallery, for instance contributing to Black History month every year. It has led the museum into new areas. A tourism development project, partly funded by the European Regional Development Fund, produced a slavery trail round Liverpool, trained a group of guides to take visitors on the tour, initiated a theatrical production for schools, a small travelling exhibition and a handling collection. The museum has held an exhibition on Haiti, its history and art, developed a project to commemorate the 50th anniversary of the arrival of Caribbean migrants on SS *Empire Windrush*, based around a specially created Caribbean garden, and hosted an exhibition on reggae!

The most important initiative has been for NML to recognize and champion UNESCO's International Day for the Remembrance of the Slave Trade and its Abolition. Beginning in 1999 with the unveiling of a commemorative plaque on the museum's quayside and the launch of a feature on the website this has grown to a three-day series of events including an international lecture series, inter-faith services, and other public events both of commemoration and celebration. Other museums and institutions are now also marking this day.

The gallery has had a significant influence elsewhere and the success of the public response has encouraged others to approach the subject. A temporary exhibition, *A Respectable Trade? Bristol and Transatlantic Slavery*, was held at the City Museum and Art Gallery in Bristol in the spring and summer of 1999, with advice and assistance from NML. By public demand, much of this exhibition was incorporated in the Industrial Museum and the story of the slave trade will be a key component in the Museum of Bristol, due to open in 2008. The National Maritime Museum in London has now addressed the subject of slavery and black seafarers in its *Trade and Empire* gallery, opened in May 1999, though not without generating a press campaign for questioning the traditional view of empire. In 2002 it added significantly to its slavery-related holdings with the purchase of the Michael Graham-Stewart Collection.

Government policy and an emphasis on broadening public access to museums, together with new funding opportunities, have also had an important effect. In 2003 a group of national and regional museums were successful in obtaining government funding for the Understanding Slavery Initiative.[11] This innovative research and development programme has provided digital and printed resources for schools and community groups and is developing training support for teachers to deal with this sensitive topic.

As 2007 and the bi-centenary of the abolition of the slave trade approaches, many museums are planning

Fig.30
Transatlantic Slavery Gallery,
Merseyside Maritime Museum, Liverpool

Fig.31
Transatlantic Slavery Gallery,
Merseyside Maritime Museum, Liverpool

Fig.32
Transatlantic Slavery Gallery,
Merseyside Maritime Museum, Liverpool

Fig.33
Maya Angelou at the opening of the
Transatlantic Slavery Gallery, October 1994

significant new initiatives. These include the ambitious National Museum and Centre for the Understanding of Transatlantic Slavery to replace the existing gallery, a new Atlantic World gallery at the National Maritime Museum, which will have slavery as a central theme and the complete re-display of the Wilberforce Museum in Hull. A number of exhibitions are planned – on Equiano in Birmingham and on abolition themes at the British Empire & Commonwealth Museum in Bristol and the National Archives in London. Other museums are looking at programming from up-dating labelling to a variety of public events and activities.

In continental Europe the situation has been rather similar. A number of museums, for instance the National Maritime Museums in Denmark and the Netherlands, have individual items or groups of items relating to the slave trade on display, but there is no comprehensive treatment of the subject or a recognition of the importance of the trade to the host countries' economic growth and development. Again there have been a number of temporary exhibitions such as the pioneering *White on Black* which was held at the Tropical Museum in Amsterdam in 1989–90. This looked at the way images of Africans and blacks were portrayed in Western popular culture and included images of slavery.[12]

A major temporary exhibition on the slave trade itself was shown at the chateau des Ducs de Bretagne in Nantes from December 1992 to February 1994.[13] Under the title *Les Anneaux de la Mémoire*, the exhibition began with an examination of the trade, then looked more closely at certain details in Nantes, Europe, Africa and the Americas, before examining abolition and the heritage of the slave trade. There was also a special display of documents related to the trade and a collection of tropical plants. The city also has two organizations dedicated to the remembrance of the slave trade and its legacies.

An exhibition based on nautical archaeological work on the slave ship *Fredensborg*, prepared by the Norwegian National Maritime Museum in Oslo, was shown there and in Denmark and Sweden in 1997 and 1998. The National Maritime Museum in Amsterdam held an exhibition in 2001–2 on the Dutch involvement in the slave trade and the activities of the West Indies Company under the title *Black Chapters: Slaves and Ships*. And most recently the Wereldmuseum in Rotterdam organized an exhibition *The heritage of slavery*. There is little evidence of the importance of the slave trade in any of the museums in the Iberian peninsula though the establishment of the Fundacion de Cultura Afrohispanoamericana in Spain in 1998 may potentially act as a stimulus.

Given the impact of the African Diaspora on the United States it is initially surprising there is no permanent exhibit on the slave trade per se in North America. Many museums now have displays which touch on slavery within local or regional historical treatments as have a number of natural history museums, which have traditionally cared for ethnographical objects. One major example is the slavery display in the American Museum of Natural History which explores the concept of slavery, but a comprehensive exploration and interpretation of the trade has not been attempted.[14] However, a major new US National Slavery Museum is planned to open in 2007 in Fredericksburg, Virginia. This will include museum displays, a library and archive and a centre for learning. Currently, the nearest developments have been at the Museum of African American History which opened in Detroit in 1997 and the National Underground Railroad Freedom Centre in Cincinnati, opened in August 2004. In Detroit the relationship between Africa and America is examined and one of three orientation areas focuses on the Middle Passage. Visitors walk over a bridge in a 70-foot replica of a slave ship and look down on cast figures representing slaves. This has proved to be controversial because the casts were taken from local schoolchildren whom critics argue are too healthy and well nourished to represent the enslaved. However, it a worthy attempt to at least engage the visitor emotionally with the centrality of the African Diaspora.[15] The Freedom Centre takes slavery as a starting point for examining the legacy of slavery and wider issues of freedom but includes relatively little about the slave trade. The exhibits include an authentic Civil War slave pen and film and multimedia presentations feature on a significant scale.

There have also been a number of temporary exhibitions in recent years which have addressed some of the aspects of the slave trade and related issues. The most pertinent is the travelling exhibit *A Slave Ship Speaks* based on the examination of the wreck of the slave ship *Henrietta Marie* and the artefacts that have been recovered. Although this seventeenth-century vessel is not characteristic of all ships employed in the slave trade, it does offer the most complete record of life on board a slaver to date.[16] The Field Museum in Chicago has also held an exhibition which included a partial reconstruction of a slave ship. Perhaps the most

Fig.34
The Slave Quarter, Carter's Grove, Virginia

comprehensive of these temporary exhibitions has been *Captive Cargoes: Transatlantic Slavery and the making of the Americas* which was organized by the Mariners' Museum, Newport News, Virginia. This was based to a considerable extent on the Transatlantic Slavery Gallery in Liverpool, making use of the research and much of the text produced by NML. The exhibition opened at Mariners' in May 2002 and has since toured to the Anacostia Museum in Washington, South Street Seaport in New York and the Missouri History Museum.

On the wider subject of slavery in the United States there have a number of important shows. Among the most comprehensive was *A House Divided: America in the Age of Lincoln* organized by the Chicago Historical Society in 1990. This placed the issue of slavery at the heart of the display and used the extensive collections of the Society, which are particularly rich in illustrative material and archival holdings.[17] In 1991 Richmond's Museum of the Confederacy addressed related issues in its exhibit *Before Freedom Came: African-American Life in the Antebellum South*. This later toured and a smaller version is incorporated in its permanent displays. Most recently, *Lest We Forget: The Triumph over Slavery*, was shown in New York in 2004 and is currently available in a travelling version.[18]

Perhaps the most ambitious programmes in the United States, or indeed anywhere, are those run by Colonial Williamsburg in Virginia.[19] Within the historic area costumed black interpreters are now an established part of the life of the town. Programs such as The Other Half tour give visitors an introduction to the lives of black Americans in eighteenth-century Williamsburg in the space of about an hour. Some of these activities have not been without controversy. A reconstruction of an auction in which slaves were sold along with other property only went ahead after bitter opposition from some local black community leaders and has not been repeated. On another occasion, white visitors have intervened on behalf of blacks being abused.[20] A major development in the spring of 1999 was the introduction of *Enslaving Virginia*, one of six programmes constituting the overriding *Becoming Americans* theme. This scrupulously researched project built on the previous work done and explores the nature of slavery and the operation of a slave economy within the Chesapeake through a wide range of interpretation and activities. However, it is noticeable that it only incidentally deals with how Africans came to be in America in the first place.

In Africa, the main interpretation of the slave trade is focused on the former castles and forts, a number of which are now preserved as historic monuments. Probably the best known are the Cape Coast Castle Museum and Elmina Castle in Ghana. There have been tensions between those responsible for the restoration, interpretation and development of the sites to cater for international tourists and those who see them as places of memory which have been desecrated. Less controversial are the Historical Museum of Ouidah and the Brazil House, the former home of an African-Brazilian family, also in Ouidah.[21] Elsewhere, the slave house on Gorée Island off Dakar, Senegal, was restored in 1990 and graphic displays were introduced in 2000. A small museum of slavery was opened at Albreda/Jufffure in The Gambia by the National Museum in June 1998. In southern Africa, the Iziko Museums in Cape Town have begun to address issues related to slavery and are currently planning to refurbish the displays within the Slave Lodge.

Several Caribbean museums have limited displays incorporating issues relating to slavery but there are desires to establish a museum of slavery in Jamaica and the museums in Barbados and Martinique would like to extend their coverage with specific galleries on the subject. The maritime museum in Bermuda is planning to introduce displays on the slave trade. The only fully developed displays on the subject are to be found at Kura Hulanda, a privately developed museum, in Curacao. Under the title *The African Holocaust* the museum examines the trade from a mainly non-European perspective and places it in the context of displays of African artefacts and replicas.

One other major international initiative is the *Slave Route* project established by UNESCO in 1993. This is attempting to stimulate recognition of the importance of the slave trade and its impact across the continents by a series of cultural and educational programmes, including conferences, exhibitions, festivals and specific work with schools and educational groups. The emphasis is on using funding and expertise in Europe to develop and stimulate activities in Africa and the Caribbean. One of the first developments has been the opening of a permanent display based on the *Fredensborg*, the Norwegian exhibition mentioned earlier, in the National Museum in Ghana.

In many museums and historic sites where there are important connections to slavery the subject matter is largely ignored. In 2002 a survey of nearly 200 plantation museums and sites in the American South concluded that slavery was almost universally ignored or trivialized. Plantations were seen in terms of their owners, the interior decoration and contents with no reference to the people whose labour produced this – the black labourers and servants. Only black-run sites and a handful of white-organized sites treated the experience of slavery adequately.[22]

There is undoubtedly a significant public interest in the history of the slave trade and slavery and a growing recognition by authorities across the continents that this needs to be acknowledged. However, despite all this activity, it remains the case that the gallery in Liverpool is the only permanent installation that attempts a comprehensive review of the history of transatlantic slavery across the three continents.

But there are difficulties in addressing and interpreting this subject for museums. Some of these are structural ones – who does it? who pays for it? where do you do it? what approach does one adopt? whose history is it? who organizes and controls the process. Some are emotional ones: it is a subject riven with potential for controversy and heartache.

In practical terms there are specific difficulties which museum professionals face. Lack of collections is one. Many British and European museums have good African collections, but mostly of nineteenth- and twentieth-century material. Generally, there is very little from the Caribbean, North or South America, particularly when related to slavery or black cultures. Most British and European museums also have little relating to their own black communities. This is partly the fault of the museums in that very few of them have attempted to engage with ethnic minorities, an essential pre-requisite to any successful collecting programme. But it may also be related to a natural suspicion of museums (which after all are generally perceived – and not inaccurately – as part of a white, middle-class establishment).[23] This is beginning to change and some museums, such as Birmingham, are beginning to develop active collecting programmes.

There are interpretative problems. For instance, many African artefacts have traditionally been seen only from a European perspective and the information recorded about them is often poor, inaccurate and partial. Very often an item is seen in terms of some notion of artistic value when in fact the social, cultural or religious aspect may be crucial.

This was highlighted in the exhibition *Africa: The Art of a Continent*, a major exhibition at the Royal Academy in London in 1995.[24]

There are few equal images. For instance, there are plenty of portraits of Liverpool slave traders but there are few representations of Africans, of any standing. Three portraits dating from 1643 of the Ambassador from Congo to Spain and two of his attendants, dressed in European finery, are outstanding exceptions. And there are almost no images by Africans themselves. The famous bronze plaques looted by the British Punitive Expedition of 1897 from the palace in Benin City are rare and treasured examples. These mostly show ceremonial life at the court of the Oba in the sixteenth and seventeenth centuries and quite a number are inspired by warfare. But whatever the messages they convey, they are African ones. And a few of the plaques are also fascinating for including Portuguese soldiers, a rare example of Africans depicting Europeans.[25] While these can be an important counter-balance to the European visual record, the circumstances of their acquisition raise other important and challenging issues.

Contemporary European images of Africa and the operation of slavery and the slave trade can be equally problematic. They need to be seen in the context within which they were created and treated with care. These illustrations often show brutality – and no one could doubt that slavery was brutal – but it is easy to slip into voyeurism, and the illustrations that accompany Stedman's *Narrative of the Surinam Revolt* may cause some unease. How valuable as an illustrative source is the famous Morland print 'The Slave Trade' which depicts an African man being forcibly separated from his wife on the beach? We need to remember that it was produced for the abolition campaign. It works on an emotional level but not as an accurate or typical record of the operation of the slave trade. And are all the figurines and prints showing Britannia 'freeing' the slaves anything more than twee souvenirs? How far do they cloud the issues of abolition and emancipation, emphasizing the humanitarian campaigns at the expense of the role of African resistance and the economic pressures? And isn't the famous illustration of the death of Captain Ferrer of the *Amistad* uncomfortably stylized and cartoon-like?

So the use of the material evidence and the messages given have to be carefully considered. They may not always be what they seem. And that applies also to the words used. Certain words and phrases can reinforce and perpetuate inappropriate attitudes. More than one museum has got itself into trouble over its labels and text.[26] In the context of slavery, it is easy to fall into the trap of using the word 'slave', with all its dehumanizing messages, to describe all Africans when there may be more accurate ways of doing so. Phrases such as 'Where did the slaves come from?' or 'How did the slaves live?' are examples and inaccurately characterize Africans without regard.

But despite the power of words, museums also have to consider the visual impact of what they present to the public. A reconstruction, an illustration, an object can convey very powerful messages and it is these visual images that visitors are likely to carry away with them and recall in the future.

So what is the way forward? It is important for museums to be more representative of the societies they serve as a whole and to reflect the interests of minorities as well as the majority. Museums also have an educative role and can play an important role in bringing difficult subjects, such as slavery, before the public at large. There are dangers; museums by their nature are clearly in the public domain and many people whether visitors, politicians, sponsors or single issue activists can have clear and distinct views of the subjects that museums address and the way that they do it. Within the area of slavery, many projects have struggled for both financial and political support and few initiatives in this field have been without some element of controversy.

But projects such as the gallery in Liverpool show that it is possible to tackle the difficult and challenging topic of transatlantic slavery and succeed. Museums do have the capacity to stimulate, to inform, educate and on occasions to move people. It is certainly worth the effort.

Notes

1 The whole question of the development and maintenance of museums in these countries is part of a wider economic infrastructure which many would see as part of the legacy of slavery and colonialism.

2 J. Peirson Jones 'The colonial legacy and the community: the Gallery 33 project', in I. Karp, C. M. Kreamer and S. D. Lavine (eds.), *Museums and Communities. The Politics of Public Culture*, Smithsonian Institution, Washington DC, 1992, pp. 221–41.

3 Marij van Helmond and Donna Palmer, *Staying Power: Black presence in Liverpool*, Liverpool, 1991.

4 Anon., *The Black Presence in Nottingham*, Nottingham City Council, 1993

5 Nick Merriman, 'The Peopling of London project', in E Hooper-Greenhill, *Cultural Diversity: Developing Museum Audiences in Britain*, Leicester, 1997, pp. 119–48.

6 Bryan Biggs (ed.), *Trophies of Empire*, Liverpool, 1992.

7 Lord Gifford, Wally Brown and Ruth Bundy, *Loosen the shackles: First report of the Liverpool 8 inquiry into race relations in Liverpool*, Liverpool, 1989.

8 For a fuller discussion on the establishment of the gallery see Anthony Tibbles, 'Against Human Dignity: The Development of the Transatlantic Slavery Gallery at Merseyside Maritime Museum, Liverpool', in Adrian Jarvis, Roger Knight and Michael Stammers (eds.), *IXth International Congress of Maritime Museums, Proceedings*, Liverpool, 1996

9 For details of the guest curators and advisory committee see p. 9.

10 For an independent review of the gallery, see Patrick Hagopian, 'Museum and exhibition reviews: Transatlantic Slavery: Against Human Dignity', *The Public Historian*, vol. 19, no. 4, 1997, pp. 102–5.

11 The museums were National Maritime Museum, National Museums Liverpool, Bristol Museums, Galleries & Archives, British Commonwealth & Empire Museum and the London regional hub.

12 It was subsequent shown in Brussels in 1991 and visited Britain, including Liverpool and Birmingham, in 1994–5. A book by the exhibition's organizer was published: Jan Nederveen Pieterse, *White on Black: Images of Africans and Blacks in Western Popular Culture*, Yale, 1992.

13 See the catalogue *Les Anneaux de la Mémoire*, Nantes, 1992

14 Edward A. Chappell, 'Museums and American Slavery', in Theresa Singleton and Mark Bogard (eds.), *Studies in African-American Archaeology*, Charlottesville, 1999.

15 Jane Lusaka, 'Finding a voice', *Museum News*, vol. 76, no. 4, July/August 1999, pp. 32–5, 68.

16 See the book based on the exhibit and the wreck site, Madeleine Burnside, *Spirits of the Passage*, New York, 1997

17 Eric Foner and Olivia Mahoney, *A House Divided: America in the Age of Lincoln*, Chicago, 1990, was published in association with the exhibit.

18 Created by The Schomberg Centre for Research in Black Culture at the New York Public Library in conjunction with UNESCO's Slave Route Project.

19 Cary Carson, 'Colonial Williamsburg and the Practice of Interpretative Planning in American History Museums', *Public Historian*, vol. 20, no. 3, 1998. See also Richard Handler and Eric Gable, *The New History in an Old Museum: Creating the Past at Colonial Williamsburg*, Durham, 1997.

20 *The Times*, London, 8 July 1999

21 For a discussion of the response within museums in Ghana and Benin to the issues of the slave trade see Theresa A. Singleton, 'The slave trade remembered on the former Gold and Slave Coasts', *Slavery and Abolition*, 20, no.1, 1999, pp. 150–69.

22 Jennifer L. Eichstedt and Stephen Small, *Representation of Slavery: Race and Ideology in Southern Plantation Museums*, Washington, DC, and London, 2002

23 Philly Desai and Andrew Thomas, *Cultural Diversity: Attitudes of Ethnic Populations Towards Museums and Galleries*, London, 1998 (prepared for Museums & Galleries Commission by BMRB International Ltd).

24 Tom Phillips (ed.), *Africa. The Art of a Continent*, London, 1995

25 Benin plaques are now found in a number of major museum collections including the British Museum in London and the Metropolitan Museum of Art in New York. For an excellent introduction to the subject and details of one of the largest collections see Kate Ezra, *Royal Art of Benin: The Perls Collection*, Metropolitan Museum of Art, New York, 1992

26 The Royal Ontario Museum experienced demonstrations and protests over its exhibition *Into the Heart of Africa* in 1990. See J. Cannizzo, *Into the Heart of Africa*, Royal Ontario Museum, Ottawa, 1990 and Helen Coxall, 'Speaking Other Voices', in E. Hooper-Greenhill, *Cultural Diversity: Developing Museum Audiences in Britain*, Leicester, 1997, pp. 99–115.

Fig.35
Oil Painting of Cape Coast Castle, John Stobart, 1958

Dear Gentleman

Sir Capt Jn[o]

Arrived at this Rivers 4 Day mar

with Berg Lines Cargo only we te

more Ivory bar and Romalls and f

and Nicanees and photes as them

first thing for our trade as We

Send Capt Burrow away with 46

460 Slaves .... I hop he

carry 460 or 460 Slaves and gh

hime wile Send by tender 34

330 Slaves I think So — as ay

may got them Cargo Ready keep

come home Dont kept home Long

I think he got Liverpoole 15 or twenth

March mind Send

Catalogue

This catalogue lists the objects on show when the gallery opened in October 1994. A number of objects were on loan from other museums for a limited period only and have now been returned.

Lenders to the Gallery

American Museum of Natural History, New York

American Numismatic Society, New York

Anti-Slavery International

Chicago Historical Society

Manchester Museum

Museum of History, Anthropology and Art of the University of Puerto Rico (Museo Universidad de Puerto Rico)

Museum of Science and Industry in Manchester

National Maritime Museum, London

Norwich Castle Museum, Norfolk Museum Service

Royal Albert Memorial Museum, Exeter

Science Museum, London

Tate & Lyle Sugars plc

Texas Memorial Museum, University of Texas at Austin (Department of History & Anthropology)

Trustees of the British Museum

Whitehaven Museum

Wilberforce House, Hull City Museums & Art Gallery

Williamson Art Gallery & Museum, Birkenhead

Origins of Transatlantic Slavery

When the Spanish first arrived on the American continent they were dazzled by the abundance of precious metals. Pre-Columbian cultures were rich in finely crafted objects made of gold and silver. Large numbers of these objects were seized and shipped back to Europe, mainly to be melted down. In fact many of the objects were made of tumbaga, an alloy of copper and gold. The Spanish took control of mining production and many of the earliest Africans to arrive in the Americas were put to work in the mines of Central and South America.

3

1 (illus. p. 18)
Part of beaker with face
Silver, Peru
124x93x130mm
NML (World Museum Liverpool)
N/N 11

2 (illus. p. 21)
Beaker, repoussé decoration of bands with scrolls and birds
Silver, Peru
115x105x156mm
NML (World Museum Liverpool)
N/N 12

3
Pair of earrings, each consisting of a hollow ring with attached flat round-shaped shield with repoussé decoration of four jaguars
Gold, Cuenca, Ecuador
192x90mm; 196x91mm
NML (World Museum Liverpool)
M13034.1-2

4 (illus. p. 21)
Figurine, tumbaga, Columbia
80x67mm
NML (World Museum Liverpool)
N/N 15

5
Nose ornament
Gold, South America
59x40mm
NML (World Museum Liverpool)
N/N 18

6 (illus. p. 18)
Scorpion
Gold, Central South America
30x21mm
NML (World Museum Liverpool)
10.10.78.43

7 (illus. p. 19)
Idol, two male figures joined at body
Tumbaga, Mexico
126x66mm
NML (World Museum Liverpool)
M13035

8
Nose ornament
Gold, Columbia
42x39mm
NML (World Museum Liverpool)
24.7.99.144

9 (illus. p. 20)
Funerary mask
Tumbaga, with vestiges of red paint with repoussé facial features, Sican culture, Peru, c.900–1500
183x305mm
NML (World Museum Liverpool)
N/N 20

10 (illus. p. 21)
Duho
Carved wood, inscription on underside 'This stool was found in a cave in the Island of Eleuthera, Bahamas about the year 1820 by James Thompson a slave and purchased of him by Theo' Pugh Wes. Miss' in 1835. It is supposed to be either a piece of the domestic furniture of the Indians or one of their Gods. It is at least 300 years old. 1850', Taino, Caribbean
355(l)x195(w)x115(h)mm
Museum of Mankind, London
1918.1

Very few objects survive from the Pre-Columbian civilizations in the Caribbean. The Taino culture of Arawaks was based principally on the island of Hispaniola and parts of Cuba and Puerto Rico.

5, 8

14

15

21

23

West African Cultures

West Africa was an area of rich and diverse societies and cultures before and during the era of transatlantic slavery. This is indicated by a small selection of objects. Although the majority date from the 19th century, they use traditional styles which exemplify earlier periods. Music was a vital part of West African life. Although individual music-making was common, music often accompanied dance and had a ceremonial and official role in many communities. A wide variety of drums, wind and stringed instruments existed.

11 (illus. p. 56)
Carving of a woman and child
Carved and painted wood, Lualli River, Cacongo, West Central Africa, 19th Century
205x163x595mm
NML (World Museum Liverpool)
24.9.00.44

12 (illus. p. 59)
Carving of a woman in a cloth skirt
Carved and painted wood, with (?)printed cotton skirt, Winneba, Ghana, 19th Century
135x120x420mm
NML (World Museum Liverpool)
13.2.09.25

13 (illus. p. 118)
Ceremonial sword
Cast handle with incised decoration terminated in the shape of a human head, and flat blade with incised decoration and animal shape, cut from sheet metal stamped 'A E ???FRITT & SONS', brass, Asante, Ghana, 19th Century
600x150x40mm
NML (World Museum Liverpool)
10.5.98.1

The stamped name on the blade indicates that it was manufactured from a sheet of brass, probably exported from Britain in the early 19th century. The general style of decoration is tradition.

14
Stool
Carved wood, Asante, Ghana
470x220x350mm
NML (World Museum Liverpool)
1977.297.2

The stool was a symbol of power and authority in Akan cultures and was widely found in both official and domestic usage.

15
Prayer board
Wood with Arabic inscription, Hausa, Nigeria
240x450mm
NML (World Museum Liverpool)
50.78.179

16 (illus. p. 104)
Comb
Carved wood, Old Calabar, Nigeria
100x245mm
NML (World Museum Liverpool)
16.6.76.24

17 (illus. p. 104)
Robe
Woven indigo dyed cotton embroidered with white cotton, Hausa, Nigeria
2440x1290mm
NML (World Museum Liverpool)
1252A

18 (illus. p. 117)
Anklet
Ivory, West Africa, (?)18th Century
123x125x30mm
NML (Merseyside Maritime Museum)
1993.137

Although frequently referred to as 'slave anklets' there is no evidence to establish a particular link with enslavement. Indeed, the value of ivory suggests that such ornaments would have belonged to wealthier members of society.

19 (illus. p. 58)
Calabash
With inscribed geometrical patterns, Rabba, Nigeria, 1860
360x330x170mm
NML (World Museum Liverpool)
20.11.60.3

20 (illus. p. 98)
Calabash
Painted with geometrical designs in red and black, Garoua, Cameroon
215x190x110mm
NML (World Museum Liverpool)
2.9.1909.20

21
Calabash
Painted with band of geometrical designs in black, Garoua, Cameroon,
215x210x110mm
NML (World Museum Liverpool)
2.9.1909.19

22 (illus. p. 106)
Bow lyre
Leather, wood and string, West Africa
200x90x610mm
NML (World Museum Liverpool)
7.7.1870.24

23
Gong, of two flattened bell shapes, joined at top and edges
Wrought iron, Calabar, Nigeria
280x230x55mm
NML (World Museum Liverpool)
16.4.61.183

24
Algiata
Wood with thin and reed mouthpiece, Missan, Nigeria
325x85x90mm
NML (World Museum Liverpool)
21.1.1925

25 (illus. p. 104)
Calabash Guitar with bow
West Africa
720x160x190mm; bow 590mm
NML (World Museum Liverpool)
22.11.24.8

26 (illus. p. 104)
Small drum with drum stick
West Africa
180(dia)x315mm; drumstick 280mm
NML (World Museum Liverpool)
65.

27
Small drum
Akim, Accra, Ghana
140(dia)x340mm
NML (World Museum Liverpool)
19.4.98.8

28 (illus. p. 94)
Trumpet
Ivory, Mandingo, Gambia
360mm
NML (World Museum Liverpool)
25.7.89.4

Early European Contact

Europeans were initially drawn to West Africa by the lure of gold. Trading in the metal was begun along the 'Gold Coast' by the Portuguese in the 15th century and was continued by English and Dutch traders in the 16th and 17th centuries. Gold was a central feature of the Asante culture and objects, particularly for adornment, were cast by highly specialized craftsmen using the lost-wax technique.

29 (illus. p. 92)
Plaque showing Bini figures
Brass, Benin, 16/17th century
330x380mm
Museum of Mankind, London
1898.1-15 no. 2

This plaque is evidence of the European presence in West Africa. Although the central figure is a Bini guard in armour, there are representations of Portuguese soldiers and of manillas, one of main trade goods, on either side of his head. The two lower figures with gong and pipes again emphasize the importance of music.

30 (illus. p. 16)
Map of Europe & North Africa
Parchment, 16th century
840x570mm
NML (Merseyside Maritime Museum)
32.99

31
Three Pendants in the form of cowrie shells
Gold, Asante, Ghana
19mm
Museum of Mankind, London
H.C. Ash 52 A-C

32
Ring
Gold, Asante, Ghana
31mm
Museum of Mankind, London
1979 AF1 4661

Gold rings were worn by royal officials on fingers and toes, often several at a time. This ring features three cannon, showing the influence of European armaments.

33
Hollow casting representing three elephants
Gold, Asante, Ghana
84mm
Museum of Mankind, London
1900 4-27 44

35

36

38

34
Pectoral disc, repoussé decoration of concentric
circles with a stylized salamander
Gold, Asante, Ghana
51mm (dia)
Museum of Mankind, London
1900 4-27 36

35
Pectoral disc, repoussé decoration featuring
stylized leaves
Gold, Asante, Ghana
90mm (dia)
Museum of Mankind, London
H.C. Ash 18

36
Pectoral disc
Gold, repoussé decoration
Gold, Asante, Ghana
39mm(dia)
NML (World Museum Liverpool)
10.10.78.45

These discs were worn by young male servants of
the Asante king on a cord around their necks. The
servants were known as 'souls' and preceded the
king on ceremonial occasions to ward off evil. The
discs are often known as soul-washers' badges.

37 (not illus.)
Sample of Gold ore
Quartz conglomerate with pyrites and native gold,
Ghana
170mm
NML (World Museum Liverpool)
1964.316.B

38
Kuduo, cylindrical base on cage-shaped stand, lid
with loop and handles decorated with birds
Brass, Asante, Ghana, c.1730-49
105(dia)x140mm
NML (World Museum Liverpool)
16.2.06.36

39 (illus. p. 100)
Kuduo, cylindrical base on cage-shaped stand
Brass, Asante, Ghana, c.1730-49
110(dia)x95mm
NML (World Museum Liverpool)
16.2.06.32

40
Kuduo, bowl with feet, and domed-shaped lid,
and central handle
Asante, Ghana, 18th century
125(dia)x150mm
NML (World Museum Liverpool)
7.3.05.1

40

41

41
Kuduo, rectangular box with lid decorated with
geometrical designs and 12 birds
Cast brass, Asante, Ghana, 18th century
77x30x30mm
NML (World Museum Liverpool)
16.2.06.39

42
Scales for measuring gold dust, of 2 circular pans
and bar with incised and punched decoration
Brass with plant fibre, Asante, Ghana
bar 120mm; dishes 52mm (dia)
NML (World Museum Liverpool)
22.10.03.21

43
Three spoons for measuring gold dust
Brass with incised decoration, Asante, Ghana
80mm; 57mm; 135mm
NML (World Museum Liverpool)
22.10.1903.17-19

44
Weights
Brass, Asante, Ghana, 17th-19th century
NML (World Museum Liverpool)

a) representing a box
   37x34x29mm
   16.2.06.45

b) representing a stool
   50x30x27mm
   59.94.4

c) rectangular
   16x14mm
   15.8.04.36

d) L-shaped
   33x32mm
   27.10.03.33

Gold dust was used as a means of exchange in
Akan societies from at least the 15th century. The
dust was stored in Kuduos, which were boxes
generally made of brass. Weighing equipment
and small brass weights were essential for
trading. The weights were produced in large
numbers and a variety of designs. The
geometrical ones are usually earlier in date than
the figurative ones.

42

43

44 a

44 b

44 c, d

Enslavement

The arrival of Europeans in West Africa brought in its wake a powerful new weapon – the gun. European firearms became an important feature of trade and it is estimated 20 million guns were exported to Africa during the slaving period. They changed the nature of warfare and raiding between different groups and assisted enslavement. Their importance is reflect in their representation in art and their use as a decorative motif.

45
Carved ivory tusk, showing chained figures
Gabon, 19th Century
340mm
NML (World Museum Liverpool)
28.2.27.30

46 (illus. p. 98)
Plaque showing European with gun
Brass, Benin, 16/17th century
170x410mm
Museum of Mankind, London
1898.1-15 no. 11

47 (illus. p. 99)
Trade gun, known as a dane gun,
18th century.
1720mm
Museum of Mankind, London
1978 AF22 843

48 (illus. p. 99)
Weights
Brass, Asante, Ghana, circa 18th century
NML (World Museum Liverpool)

a) representing a man with gun
40x28mm
1974.30.24

b) representing a gun
65mm
7.3.05.87

c) representing a cannon
95x20mm
50.78.354

49 (illus. p. 102)
Yoke
Wood, 19th century, West Africa
1745mm
Anti-Slavery International
MH LI 93-4

50 (illus. p. 94)
War trumpet
Ivory, Congo, 19th Century
670mm
NML (World Museum Liverpool)
29.7.1901.2

45

51

Trading and Trade Goods

Europeans exported a wide range of items to trade for slaves, often responding to African demands for particular goods. They were mostly manufactured goods with practical applications, like firearms or textiles. Some items, such as cowries and manillas, could be used as currency and others had a decorative function, like beads.

61

51
Map of West African coast with inset of Goree Island, 'Carte Particuliere / Des Costes de / L'Afrique / Qui comprehend le Royaume de Cacheo le Province de Gelofo etc / Levee Par Ordere Expres des Roys de Portugal sous qui ou en a Fait la Decouverte / A Amsterdam / chez Pierre Mortier Libraire /....',
Pierre Mortier, Amsterdam, 1693
395x530mm
National Maritime Museum, London
241 2/1

52 (illus. p. 96)
Map of Congo & Angola, 'Regna / Congo / et / Angola',
John Ogilby, 1670
330x275mm
National Maritime Museum, London
241 6/1

53 (illus. p. 97)
Map of Africa, printed, coloured, 'Africam Graeci Libyam App: / AFRICAE TABVLA NOVA / Edita Antverpiae 1570'
Probably from Ortelius, Theatrum Orbis Terrarum, Antwerp, 1570
480x365mm
National Maritime Museum, London
G290 1/10

54 (illus. p. 74)
'An Accurate / MAP of / AFRICA / from the Best / Authorities'
'Engrav'd for the Beauties of Nature and Art display'd. Printed for G. Robinson, in Pater-noster Row, London / V.g.p.139', 18th century
235x201mm
NML (Merseyside Maritime Museum)
1976.291

55 (illus. p. 15)
Trade token
Ivory, inscribed 'Tom Buck of Grandy Bonny an Honest Trader he sold me 20 Slaves Ship Liverpool'
133mm(dia)
NML (Merseyside Maritime Museum)
1961.57

56 (illus. p. 26)
Trade token
Ivory, inscribed JOHN PEPPER BRIG HIGHFIELD A GOOD MAN'
95mm(dia)
NML (World Museum Liverpool)
4427M

The exact significance and use of these tokens has not been established but they were presumably exchanged as pledges or receipts.

57 (not illus.)
Two Lead shot bags
Hessian, printed with Royal Coat of Arms 'PATENT SHOT NEWTON, KEATES & Co. LEAD MERCHANTS. LIVERPOOL No. 5' AND 'No. 6' No. 5 281x165mm; No. 6 265x163mm
NML (Merseyside Maritime Museum)
1986.201

Arms and ammunition were one of the most important items exported to West Africa, not least because of their impact on the nature of warfare.

58 (illus. p. 27)
Head-dress of cowrie shells with roan antelope horns
Kon Kombo, West Africa
580x430x285mm
NML (World Museum Liverpool)
56.25.161

59 (illus. p. 28)
String of cowrie shells
West Africa.
850mm
NML (World Museum Liverpool)
11.2.18.11

Cowries came originally from the Maldive Islands in the Indian Ocean and mainly reached Africa on slave ships via Ceylon and Amsterdam. They were used as currency in many areas of West Africa but were also used in decorative ways as a reflection of wealth and position.

60 (illus. p. 28)
Necklace, of hollow tubes of coiled wire
Brass, Muni River, Eloby, West Africa
135(dia)x85mm
NML (World Museum Liverpool)
19.4.98.55

61
Bracelet, of continuous tube of coiled wire
Brass
80(dia)x250mm
NML (World Museum Liverpool)
51.68.738

62
Gin bottle
Green glass, square sided, with 'v HOYTEMA & C.' moulded in glass, Dutch, 18th century
National Maritime Museum, London

This bottle was found on the New Calabar River, near Iba, in present-day Nigeria. Alcohol was one of the main items exported to West Africa by British and European traders.

62

63
String of yellow glass beads with green, red and
blue 'tartan' decoration
255mm
NML (World Museum Liverpool)
51.68.546

64
String of yellow glass beads with green, red and
blue decoration
Venetian, from Krobo, Ghana
110mm
NML (World Museum Liverpool)
51.68.775

65
Yellow glass bead, with green and red decoration
Krobo, Ghana
23mm
NML (World Museum Liverpool)
1980.108.8

66 (not illus.)
String of clear, white, black, red and green glass
beads, with white, yellow and red decoration
210mm
NML (World Museum Liverpool)
46.35.54

67
String of coral beads
Benin
370mm
NML (World Museum Liverpool)
42.11

68
Glass bead, white with blue and brown
geometrical decoration
Venetian, from Northern Nigeria
42mm
NML (World Museum Liverpool)
N/N89

69
String of agate, Cambray type and Indian glass
beads from a wreck of a ship, off St Agnes, Isles
of Scilly
130mm
NML (World Museum Liverpool)
1987.9.1-4

70
Trade beads
250mm
NML (World Museum Liverpool)
1992.05.19

71
String of Levine glass beads
Bethnal Green, London
400mm
NML (World Museum Liverpool)
56.29.603

72
String of cornaline dialleppo pink & white beads
445mm
NML (World Museum Liverpool)
N/N

Glass beads were a regular cargo. In the 1770s
they made up between 25% and 50% of the value
of cargoes shipped by the Liverpool merchant
William Davenport to the Cameroons. Davenport
also supplied other slave traders and in 1766-70
sold beads worth about £39,000. Many beads
came from Venice but increasingly they were
made in many other parts of Western Europe.

73 (illus. p. 29)
Four Queen Manillas
Copper
NML (World Museum Liverpool)

a) 285x140mm
   28.3.07.15

b) 270x120mm
   28.3.07.16

c) 270x120mm
   1991.41.2

d) 235x170mm
   26.6.11.23

74
Three Small Manillas
Copper alloy
NML (World Museum Liverpool)

a) 60x60mm
   46.47

b) 106x95mm
   32.103.3

c) 100x90mm
   32.103.2

75
Two Small Manillas
Brass
NML (World Museum Liverpool)

a) 66x68mm
   1942.18

b) 60x60mm
   1942.18

Manillas are horseshoe-shaped bracelets of
brass or copper which were used as a form of
currency particularly in the Niger delta. They
were manufactured in European foundries and
were frequently used as a source of metal for
casting in Africa.

70, 65, 63
64

67

71
68, 69
72

74, 75

76 (not illus.)
Clay pipe, English, 18th century
NML (Merseyside Maritime Museum)

Clay pipes were exported throughout the slaving
period and fragments have been found in many
parts of West Africa. They were also no doubt
used by resident European traders.

77
Sample of brocaded silk, c.1770-80
480x930mm
NML (Walker Art Gallery)
1988.20.19.b

Cloth was the largest single item exported to
Africa. Fashions in demand varied on different
parts of the coast and at different times. Some
cloths were standard woollens from England and
Flanders, or linens from the Netherlands and
Silesia. There was also a significant demand for
more luxurious silks and cottons from India.
Later European imitations of Indian cloths were
produced.

77

European Traders

The merchants who organized the slave trade were often prosperous and respected members of their communities. Their activities were regarded as beneficial to their fellow citizens. The ships they used are represented in a number of contemporary art forms which are important documentary sources.

78 (illus. p. 70)
Guinea
Gold, Royal African Company, 1663
Obverse, Bust of King and Elephant, 'CAROLVS II DEI GRATIA', Reverse Royal arms, 'MAG BR FRA ET HIB REX 1663'
British Museum
E1528

79
Guinea
Gold, Royal African Company, 1665
Obverse, Bust of King and Elephant, 'CAROLVS II DEI GRATIA', Reverse Royal arms, 'MAG BR FRA ET HIB REX 1665'.
British Museum
Banks v.1p.75

80
5 Guineas
Gold, Royal African Company, 1668
Obverse, Bust of King and Elephant, 'CAROLVS II DEI GRATIA', Reverse Royal arms, 'MAG BR FRA ET HIB REX 1668'
British Museum
Grueber 720

81
5 Guineas
Gold, Royal African Company, 1669
Obverse, Bust of King and Elephant, 'CAROLVS II DEI GRATIA', Reverse Royal arms, 'MAG BR FRA ET HIB REX 1669'
British Museum
E1509

The British Royal African Company had a monopoly of trade to Africa until 1698. It had the privilege of having coins struck at the mint from metal which it imported. The gold came from Guinea and the name was transferred to the coin.

82 (illus. p. 71)
Thomas Golightly
19th century British School, oil on canvas
890x692mm
NML (Walker Art Gallery)
7001

Thomas Golightly (1732-1821) was a leading Liverpool merchant and civic leader. He was elected to the Council in 1770 and served as Bailiff (1770), Mayor (1772-3) and was a Senior Member and Treasurer (1789-1820). He was also a Justice of the Peace from 1779. He was involved in the slave trade and he is listed among 'the Company of Merchants trading to Africa' in 1807.

83 (not illus.)
Goblet
Glass painted in enamel colours with Royal Coat of Arms and on the reverse a depiction of a 3 masted ship and the inscription 'Success to the African trade of WHITE-HAVEN' and signed 'Beilby juvt invt & pinxt', by William Beilby (1740-1819), Newcastle upon Tyne, c.1762-63
250mm high
Whitehaven Museum

This is one of a small number of goblets bearing the Royal coat of arms produced by William Beilby and which used the technique he discovered in 1761 to fuse enamel on to glass. The other surviving goblets all feature the Prince of Wales' device on the reverse. This goblet was almost certainly produced to commemorate the vessel *King George* which was built in Whitehaven in 1762-3 for the slave trade. John Paul Jones, 'the founder of the American Navy', was third mate on the maiden voyage.

84 (illus. p. 33)
Grand Turk
Exhibition model by W. G. Leavitt, of Salem, Massachusetts, Scale 1:48
NML (Merseyside Maritime Museum)
1952.1

This brig of about 300 tons was built at Wiscasset, Maine, in the USA in 1812 and was purchased by a group of merchants from Salem who gave her the name *Grand Turk*. She was used in privateering, particularly against the British, with whom the Americans were at war from 1812-15. Although pierced for 18 guns, the model only shows 16. The vessel is typical of the fine-lined vessels which were used in slave trading.

79

80

81

85 (illus. p. 35)
Watt
Contemporary builders' model, 1797, Scale 1:24
Williamson Art Gallery & Museum, Birkenhead
82.186

The *Watt*, built by Edward Grayson of Liverpool
for the firm of Watt & Walker, was launched in
February 1797. She was a 22-gun ship-rigged
vessel of 564 tons. The firm's main business was
in trade with Jamaica, where the Watt family also
had an estate, and the vessel was mainly
employed bringing back sugar from Jamaica.

86 (illus. p. 35)
Ship bowl, 'Success To The Dobson'
Depiction of ship painted in under glazed blue,
enamelled in red and green, tin-glazed
earthenware, Liverpool, 1770
270(dia)x110mm
NML (Walker Art Gallery)
50.60.13

The *Dobson* was a 200 ton ship built in Liverpool
in 1770. Her principal shareholder was William
Davenport, one of the most active slave traders in
the port, who invested in some 120 slave voyages
during a career of nearly 40 years.

87 (illus. p. 36)
A Liverpool Slave Ship
About 1780, by William Jackson, (active about
1780-1803), oil on canvas
1040x1090mm, signed 'W. Jackson Pnx'
NML (Merseyside Maritime Museum)
1964.227.2

This unidentified 16-gun ship is typical of the
vessels used in the slave trade. She is shown in a
port profile against a wooded coastline, intended
to represent West Africa. The ship is about to
drop anchor and a boat is to be launched. The
ventilation holes below her gun deck suggest she
is intended to carry slaves. Recent cleaning has
revealed three small boats with Africans on board
approaching from the coast.

88 (illus. p. 32)
Armed Brig in the Mersey
About 1810, by John Jenkinson (active 1790-
1821), oil on canvas
810x1120mm, signed 'J. Jenkinson'
NML (Merseyside Maritime Museum)
1991.5

Although this 14-gun brig is unidentified, she is
typical of the large merchant vessels which were
involved in slaving from Liverpool. The Liverpool
Guide of 1796 comments 'The Guineamen [slave
traders] here, are in general the handsomest
ships; being every way modelled after the
Frigates, and rather more ornamented.' The ship
is shown in a starboard view in the Mersey off the
Wirral coast, near Birkenhead.

The Middle Passage

The Middle Passage was a dehumanizing
experience, characterized by fear and
brutality. Male Africans were shackled below
deck and men, women and children were
subject to punishment and abuse.

89
Shackles, neck iron and chains
Wrought iron, 18th century
NML (Merseyside Maritime Museum)
N/N

90
Shackles, leg irons
Wrought iron, 18th century
295mm
NML (World Museum Liverpool)
1956.26.709

91
Shackles, leg irons
Wrought iron, 18th century
400mm
NML (World Museum Liverpool)
56.24.135

92 (not illus.)
Cat-o'-nine-tails
Nine knotted cords, with wooden handle covered
with green and red baize
1143mm, late 19th century
National Maritime Museum, London

Although this is an example of a later Royal Naval
Cat-o'nine tails, it is identical to the sort used on
board vessels during the slaving period.

93 (illus. p. 41)
Grape shot in bag
Lead, 18th century
NML (Merseyside Maritime Museum)
1986.201.84B

94 (illus. p. 99)
Flintlock blunderbuss
Late 18th century
810mm
NML (World Museum Liverpool)
60.86.1

95 (not illus.)
Chart of the Atlantic, with a voyage of a slave
ship, 1794
540x1410mm
NML (Merseyside Maritime Museum)
OA 1866

96 (illus. p. 43)
Log book of the 'Unity'
1769-71
210x175mm
NML (Merseyside Maritime Museum)
1993.108

This log covers a slaving voyage of the *Unity* from
Liverpool to Cape Coast Castle and Jamaica,
returning to Liverpool in May 1771. She was
owned by the Earle family, who were important
merchants in Liverpool in the 18th and 19th
centuries. Although they traded to the
Mediterranean and elsewhere much of their
business involved the slave trade and plantation
goods from the West Indies.

97 (illus. p. 41)
Necklace of nine charm pendants
Cloth, leather and horn, Mandingo, Gambia
640mm
NML (World Museum Liverpool)
13.2.69.7

98 (illus. p. 29)
Surgical instrument set, cased, by Whitford
London, late 18th/early 19th century
455x222mm
Science Museum, London
A600582

Surgeons were carried on many slave ships,
though their abilities varied greatly. Most of their
work involved examining captives and dealing
with disease. They would rarely have had
recourse to their instruments.

89

90

91

99

101

Destinations

The majority of enslaved Africans were taken to the Caribbean, where England, France and the other European participants all had colonies by the end of the 17th century. Equally large numbers were also taken to Brazil, particularly in the 19th century. Spanish colonies in Central and South America were an important destination in the early years of slavery. Only about 1 in 20 Africans were taken directly to the Southern states of North America.

99
'A / GENERAL CHART / OF / THE WEST INDIA ISLANDS / WITH THE ADJACENT COASTS OF / THE SPANISH CONTINENT, / BY L. S. DE LA ROCHETTE. / M.DCCXCVI. / LONDON. / PUBLISHED BY W. FADEN GEOGRAPHER TO THE KING / AND TO H.R.H. THE PRINCE OF WALES, / SEPTEMBER 22D 1796', printed coloured chart, 1796
623x880mm
NML (Merseyside Maritime Museum)
1992.141

100 (illus. p. 23)
Chart of Caribbean & Gulf of Mexico, printed coloured chart, 'Insulae / Americanae / in Oceano Septemtrionali ac / Regiones Adiacentes / ac de May usque ad Lineam equinoctialem / Par Nicolaum Visscher / Cum Privilegio Ordinum Hollandaise et Westfrisiae' by Nicolas Visscher, Amsterdam, c.1700
540x435mm
National Maritime Museum, London
G245 1/8

101
Map of Caribbean & Gulf of Mexico, printed chart, 'Carte Reduite / du GOLPHE DU MEXIQUE / et des INDES DE L'AMERIQUE ....Seconde edition Annee 17.....Par le S. Bellin', by Jacques Nicolas Bellin, Paris, 1770
805x535mm
National Maritime Museum, London
G245 1/14

102
Map of Caribbean, printed chart, 'Pascaerte vande / CARIBES /....', by Johannes Van Keulen, Amsterdam, 1st half 18th century
580x510mm
National Maritime Museum, London
245 2/2

102

103 (illus. p. 53)
Plan of Havana, with inset map of Cuba, printed,
'An exact plan of the / City, Fortifications &
Harbour of / Havana / in the Island of Cuba /
From an original Drawing taken on the Spot /
Universal Magazine, J. Hinton, Newgate Street.',
by John Hinton, from the *Universal Magazine*,
London, c.1762
340x255mm
National Maritime Museum, London
G245 6/10

104 (illus. p. 46)
Map of St Domingue, printed chart, 'Carte de
L'ISLE DE SAINT DOMINIQUE.....Par le Sr.
Bellin....1764', by Jacques Nicolas Bellin, Paris,
1764
905x570mm
National Maritime Museum, London
245 8/13

105 (illus. p. 46)
Map of Jamaica divided into parishes, printed
chart, 'DESCRIPTIO per JOHANNEM OGILIUM
Cosmographum Regium 1761', by John Ogilby,
1671
520x415mm
National Maritime Museum, London
245 11/3

106 (illus. p. 23)
Map of the Virgin Islands, printed coloured chart,
'THE VIRGIN ISLANDS / from / ENGLISH and
DANISH SURVEYS / BY / THOMAS JEFFERYS /
Geographer to the King', by Thomas Jefferys,
printed and published by Robert Sayer, 1775
590x442mm
National Maritime Museum, London
G245 14/7

108

109

107 (illus. p. 24)
Map of Curacao, printed chart with plan, elevation and 6 views, 'Nieuwe Afteekening / van het Eyland / Curacao / vertoonende alle desselfs geleegentheedom / mitsgaders de haven van / St. Anna en't Fort Amsterdam / Int grood als ook hoe sig dit Eyland / uyt der zee vertoont / Tot Amsterdam by / Gerard van Keulen', by Gerard Van Keulen, Amsterdam, 1st quarter of 18th century
590x390mm
National Maritime Museum, London
G245 15/14

108
Map of Martinique, printed chart with inset of harbour of Cul de Sae Marin, 'Carte Reduit de / L'ISLE DE MARTINIQUE......Par M. Bellin.....1758', by Jacques Nicolas Bellin, Paris, 1758
880x560mm
National Maritime Museum, London
245 15/33

109
Map of Guadeloupe, printed chart , 'Carte Reduit des ISLES DE / LA GUADELOUPE / MARIE GALANTE ET LES SAINTES...Par le Sr. Bellin ....1759', by Jacques Nicolas Bellin, Paris, 1759
870x580mm
National Maritime Museum, London
245 15/34

110 (illus. p. 24)
Map of St Lucia, printed chart with insets of Carenage, Cul de Sac des Roseaux and Grand Islet et du choc, 'Carte de / L'ISLE DE SAINTE LUCIE / Par le Sr. Bellin....1763', by Jacques Nicolas Bellin, 1763
880x560mm
National Maritime Museum, London
G245 15/35

111
Coloured facsimile map of St Kitts & Nevis, 'An Accurate Map of the Islands of St Christophers and Nevis in the West Indies, By an Officer, With the Position of the English and French fleets, February 7th 1782 / Published April 1, 1782, by I. Fielding, Pater noster Row; J. Sewell, Cornhill; and J. Debrett, Piccadilly', 1782
310x375mm
National Maritime Museum, London
G345 15/3

112
24 Shilling Piece,Silver, Danish West Indies, 1764
Obverse: crowned double monogram of Frederick V 'D G DAN NOR VAN GOT REX', Reverse: image of ship, 'XXIIII SKILL DANSKE AMERICANSK M 1764'
NML (World Museum Liverpool)
15.2.89.290

111

119
Half-penny Token, Copper, Barbados, 1788
Obverse: image of a head 'I SERVE', Reverse:
image of a pineapple 'BARBADOES HALF-PENNY
1788'
NML (World Museum Liverpool)
N/N

These tokens are the earliest minted coins from
Barbados, probably struck by order of Sir Philip
Gibbs, a plantation owner. They were designed by
John Milton but were never recognized as legal
colonial coinage.

120
One Stiver, Demarary & Essequebo, copper, 1813
Obverse: bust of king, 'GEORGIUS III D.G. REX',
Reverse: crown and oak leaves, 'COLONIES OF
ESSEQUEBO AND DEMERARY TOKEN 1813 ONE
STIVER'
NML (World Museum Liverpool)
N/N

121
Section of Coin, stamped with emblem, silver,
Curacao, Dutch West Indies, 1807-15
NML (World Museum Liverpool)
N/N

122
Section of Coin, stamped with emblem, Curacao,
Dutch West Indies, 1807-15
NML (World Museum Liverpool)
N/N

123
Cut Silver, stamped with emblem, St Lucia
NML (World Museum Liverpool)
1966.300.194

124
Seal, wax, Royal coat of arms of George III,
'OFFICE FOR REGISTRATION OF SLAVES
DEMERARY', Demerara.
274x205mm
NML (Merseyside Maritime Museum)
51.111

125 (illus. p. 49)
Auction Hammer, ivory with silver band, ?19th
century
32mm(dia)x125mm
Whitby Museum

113 (illus. p. 52)
24 shilling piece, Danish West Indies, 1767
Obverse: monogram of Christian VII 'D G DAN
NOR VAN GOT REX', Reverse: image of ship, 'XII
SKILL DANSKE AMERICANSK M 1767'
NML (World Museum Liverpool)
15.2.89.91

114
12 Shilling Piece, Danish West Indies, 1767
Obverse: monogram of Christian VII 'D G DAN
NOR VAN GOT REX', Reverse: image of ship, 'XII
SKILL DANSKE AMERICANSK M 1767'
NML (World Museum Liverpool)
15.2.89.292

115
12 Shilling Piece, Danish West Indies, 1767
Obverse: monogram of Christian VII 'D G DAN
NOR VAN GOT REX', Reverse: image of ship, 'XII
SKILL DANSKE AMERICANSK M 1767'
NML (World Museum Liverpool)
15.2.89.293

116 (illus. p. 48)
One Penny Token, Copper, Barbados, 1788
Obverse: image of a head 'I SERVE', Reverse:
image of a pineapple, 'BARBADOES PENNY 1788'
NML (World Museum Liverpool)
N/N

117
One Penny Token, Copper, Barbados, 1788
Obverse: image of a head 'I SERVE', Reverse:
image of a pineapple, 'BARBADOES PENNY 1788'
NML (World Museum Liverpool)
1966.300.196

118
One Penny Token, Copper, Barbados, 1792
Obverse: image of a head 'I SERVE', Reverse.
image of Neptune, 'BARBADOES PENNY 1792'
NML (World Museum Liverpool)
N/N

112

114

117

115

118

119

121

122

120

123

Slave Life in the Americas

There are relatively few objects directly
associated with the lives of slaves. Many of
these are instruments of torture and
punishment. Slaves themselves had few
possessions. In maroon communities
craftsmen produced a wider range of items
that were necessary to sustain everyday life.
Music and dance played an important part
and the continuity of an African tradition can
be seen in a small selection of instruments.

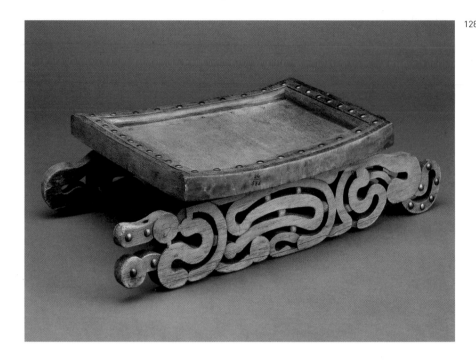
128

126 (illus. p. 127)
The TOBACCO MANUFACTORY in different
branches, Engrav'd for the *Universal Magazine*
1750 for J. Hinton at the Kings Arms in St Pauls
Church Yard London, Engraving, laid off white
paper and black ink
203x245mm
NML (Merseyside Maritime Museum)
1994.21

Tobacco was another labour-intensive crop but
which also required skilled handling, particularly
in the drying and finishing processes depicted
here. Tobacco was mainly grown in North
America, especially in Virginia and Maryland, but
was also cultivated in Brazil.

127 (not illus.)
Stool, carved wood with snake motif, Saramaccer
tribe, Ganya Condree Valley, Upper Surinam
River, Dutch Guiana
241x311x330mm
American Museum of Natural History, New York
26.203

128
Grinding Board, for mashing peanuts, carved
wood, Aucaner tribe, Moompusu Village,
Tapanahoni River, Dutch Guiana
140x489x349mm
American Museum of Natural History, New York
26.588

129
Comb, wood with bird motif, Aucaner tribe, Lassa
Bakka River, Sara Creek District, Dutch Guiana
343x410x13mm
American Museum of Natural History, New York
26.414

Wood-carving is an important feature of the
maroon communities of Dutch Guiana and a wide
range of objects were produced. While many
items are similar to those found in Africa,
decorative wood-carving only began in the early
19th century and its development was not derived
directly from African traditions or styles.

130
Bread bowl, carved wood, ?19th century
Texas Memorial Museum,

131 (not illus.)
Rolling pin, carved wood, ?19th century
Texas Memorial Museum,

132
Drum, wood, cedar root and deer skin, Virginia,
late 17th century
290(dia)x410mm
Museum of Mankind, London
SL1368

132

This Asante-style drum was acquired by Sir Hans
Sloane (1660-1753) in Virginia. As a physician and
naturalist he travelled widely in the American
colonies. The drum is an example of how cultural
traditions were transferred from Africa to the
Americas.

133 (illus. p. 32)
Drum, 'The Nanda', Paramacca tribe , Seeton
Ponta Village, Marowyne River, French Guiana
267x438(dia)mm
American Museum of Natural History, New York
26.544

134
Marimbola, wood with red, black and white
painting, Loiza Aldea, Puerto Rico, 1950
445x595x173mm
Museo Universidad de Puerto Rico

134

135
Drum, wood with red black and yellow painting,
rope and leather, Loiza Aldea, Puerto Rico 1950
432(dia)x445mm
Museo Universidad de Puerto Rico

These instruments demonstrate that the
continuity of African traditions among slave and
former slave communities has lasted through
until the present day.

136
Neck shackle, wrought iron, 19th century
560x343mm
Museo Universidad de Puerto Rico

137
Poster advertising for a runaway slave, St Louis,
23 August 1852
290x460mm
Hull Museums
24/52

138 (illus. p. 111)
Punishment collar, wrought iron, 18th century
188(dia)x310mm
Manchester Museum
0.9322/289

139 (illus. p. 128)
Slave badge, copper alloy, stamped
'CHARLESTON / 1392 / SERVANT / 1846', 1846
American Numismatic Society, New York
0000.999.37277

In the early 19th century, slaves in Charleston,
South Carolina, were required to register their
names and occupations and wear an identity
badge. In 1848 this requirement was also
extended to free black people.

140
Shackles, wrought iron
Chicago Historical Society

141 (illus. p. 63)
Letter to Thomas Eaton, Swansea, from his slave,
Pheba in Kingston, Jamaica, 12 March 1793
305x186mm
Hull Museums
Box 7/18

Pheba writes to complain about ill-treatment she
and her daughter have suffered when hired out.

130

135

136

139

137

☞ $2,500 ☜
REWARD!

RANAWAY, from the Subscriber, residing in Mississippi county, Mo., on Monday the 5th inst., my

Negro Man named GEORGE.

Said negro is five feet ten inches high, of dark complexion, he plays well on the Violin and several other instruments. He is a shrewd, smart fellow and of a very affable countenance, and is twenty-five years of age. If said negro is taken and confined in St. Louis Jail, or brought to this county so that I get him, the above reward of $1,000 will be promptly paid.

JOHN MEANS.

Also, from Radford E. Stanley,

A NEGRO MAN SLAVE, NAMED NOAH,

Full 6 feet high; black complexion; full eyes; free spoken and intelligent; will weigh about 180 pounds; 32 years old; had with him 2 or 3 suits of clothes, white hat, short blue blanket coat, a pair of saddle bags, a pocket compass, and supposed to have $350 or $400 with him.

ALSO---A NEGRO MAN NAMED HAMP,

Of dark copper color, big thick lips, about 6 feet high, weighs about 175 pounds, 36 years old, with a scar in the forehead from the kick of a horse; had a lump on one of his wrists and is left-handed. Had with him two suits of clothes, one a casinet or cloth coat and grey pants.

Also, Negro Man Slave named BOB,

Copper color, high check bones, 5 feet 11 inches high, weighs about 150 pounds, 22 years old, very white teeth and a space between the centre of the upper teeth Had a blue blanket sack coat with red striped linsey lining. Supposed to have two suits of clothes with him; is a little lame in one ancle.

$1,000 will be given for George----$600 for Noah---$450 for Hamp--$450 for Bob; if caught in a free State, or a reasonable compensation if caught in a Slave State, if delivered to the Subscribers in Miss. Co., Mo., or confined in Jail in St. Louis, so that we get them   Refer to

**JOHN MEANS &
R. E. STANLEY.**

ST. LOUIS, August 23, 1852.   (PLEASE STICK UP.)

140

142 (illus. p. 45)
Punishment Records, Friendship Plantation,
Jamaica, January–June 1828
355x475mm
Hull museums
46.72

Records of punishments were kept on many
plantations. They listed not only the name and
offence but the time, place, extent of the
punishment and by whom authorized and
inflicted.

143 (illus. p. 61)
Receipt from Court of Baltimore to Mr R.
O'Ferrale for payment of $1000 for female slaves,
Baltimore, 5 September 1859
Hull Museums
Box 10/15

European Rewards

A range of raw materials were imported into Europe which were directly produced by slave labour or were paid for from the profits of the slavery. Wealthy Europeans in the 18th and early 19th centuries were surrounded with reminders of transatlantic slavery whether by the sugar on their tables or the mahogany chairs they sat on. The huge scale of production also brought many items, like sugar, within reach of the poor.

144 (not illus.)
'Plan of the City of Bristol and its Suburbs', showing sugar refineries, commenced 1813 by John Plumley and completed by George C. Ashmead, 1828
Bristol Museums & Art Gallery
M766

145
Two sugar loaves
515x130(dia) mm; 270x120(dia)mm
Tate & Lyle, London

146
Sugar breaker, cast iron, 'SYMES PATENT / LONDON', 19th century
380x640mm
Tate & Lyle, London

147
Sugar bowl, china, white ground with gilt decoration, c.1800
113(dia)x117mm
NML (Walker Art Gallery)
55.20.16

148
Sugar nippers, late 18th/early 19th century
NML (Walker Art Gallery)
1969.216.7

149
Tea pot, china, white ground with gilt decoration, c.1800
139x88mm
NML (Walker Art Gallery)
55.20.14

150
Coffee pot, creamware, transfer printed in black with scene of couple seated in garden being served by a black servant, Liverpool, c.1760-5
109(dia)x215mm
NML (Walker Art Gallery)
1980.24.2

149, 147

146, 145

148

150

151

151
Coffee cup, porcelain, transfer printed in black
with scene of couple seated in garden being
served by a black servant, Liverpool, c.1760-5
38(dia)x62mm
NML (Walker Art Gallery)
59.119.107

Sugar was the most important of the raw
materials brought back to Europe, where it was
refined and sold. It was used to sweeten the
naturally bitter beverages, like coffee and tea,
and made them hugely popular. As one early 19th
century dictionary put it, sugar was "one of the
indispensable necessaries of life."

152 (illus. p. 69)
Punch pot, earthenware, black ground hand
painted with gilt decoration, 'IAM + GIBLET /
1766', 1766
NML (Walker Art Gallery)
M1240-1

153
Pepper pot, pewter, late 18th century
63(dia)x109mm
NML (Walker Art Gallery)
N/N

Although most pepper came from the East, it was
also grown in the Americas and regularly figures
as a cargo on ships returning to Europe.

154
Knife and fork with ivory handles,
276mm; 252mm
NML (Walker Art Gallery)
N/N

Ivory was widely used as handles for cutlery from
the 17th century and although much of it came
from the Indian sub-continent, Africa remained
an important source.

153

155

154

155
Glass bottle containing ginger powder, with
printed label 'PREPARED POWDER / OF /
JAMAICAN GINGER'
66(dia)x205mm
NML (Merseyside Maritime Museum)
1986.201.7c

Ginger was an important spice which was grown
on many Caribbean islands and was regularly
used by European cooks. This sample, probably
dating from the early 19th century, was part of a
collection of items preserved by the Wynn family
of North Wales.

156 (not illus.)
Chair, mahogany, English, c.1730-40
971mm high
NML (Lady Lever Art Gallery)
LL4346

157 (not illus.)
Bracket clock, satinwood,
281x164x421mm
NML (Lady Lever Art Gallery.)
LL4461

158 (not illus.)
Knife box, mahogany, English, early 19th century
204x222x309mm
NML (Lady Lever Art Gallery)
LL4793

159
Wood samples, 9 samples of cedar, brasiletto,
fustic, logwood, camphor, lignum vitae,
satinwood, pimento wood and mahogany.
56x30mm
NML (Walker Art Gallery)
1986.149

When mahogany was introduced into Britain in
the early 18th century, it was known as Jamaica
wood because the island was then the principal
source. It became the most popular wood for
furniture making and was also used for doors,
panelling and other interior details into the 19th
century. Supplies were obtained from many parts
of Central and South America, including
Honduras and Cuba. Other American woods, such
as satinwood, were used as inlay and decoration.

160
Dye recipe book, 1821
Museum of Science & Industry, Manchester

Other timbers, such as logwood and fustic, were
imported from the Caribbean and Central
America. They were used as dyes in the textile
industry and as stains in furniture making.

159

Black People in Europe

Although the number of Africans in Europe was small in relation to the millions who were transported to the Americas, there was a significant black presence in all Western European countries. They are, however, only rarely represented in contemporary paintings and illustrations.

161 (illus. p. 78)
Olaudah Equiano, British School, late 18th Century
Royal Albert Memorial Museum, Exeter

Equiano (about 1743-1797) is one of the few Africans whose personal story and experience of being enslaved has come down to us, through his autobiography, published in 1789. After his escape from slavery, he settled in London and was an active campaigner against the slave trade. He toured throughout Britain speaking against slavery. This is the only known portrait of the man who was perhaps the best known African in Britain in the 18th century.

162
'The Interesting Narrative of the life of Olaudah Equiano, or Gustavus Vassa, the African. Written by himself', 6th Edition, London, 1793
173x113mm
NML (Merseyside Maritime Museum)

163 (illus. p. 81)
The Black Boy, by William Windus, (1822-1907), oil on canvas
761x635mm
NML (Walker Art Gallery)
1601

This young African boy is said to have come to Liverpool as a stowaway and was engaged by Windus as an errand boy. It is reputed to have been painted in 1844 and thus the boy probably came to Liverpool on a vessel carrying palm oil. There were other Africans in the port at this time, mainly as a result of the trade with West Africa and the employment of Africans as crewmen.

164
Tile 'The Turkish Merchant', Tin-glazed earthenware transfer printed in black, Liverpool, 126x126mm
NML (Walker Art Gallery)
15.12.20.16

160

162

164

166

Abolition & Emancipation.

The campaigns for the abolition of the slave trade and the emancipation from slavery were popular subjects for the producers of commemorative china and of tokens and medals.

165 (illus. p. 44)
Figure of an enslaved African breaking free of his chains, carved wood, American, late 19th century
1900mm high
NML (Merseyside Maritime Museum)
1993.170

This full-sized figure is similar to other carved figures in the American folk art tradition. An enslaved African is represented in the act of breaking free of his chains in what may be seen as a symbolic gesture.

166
Epistles from the yearly meeting of Friends, 16??-1817, Published London, 1818
230x150mm
NML (Merseyside Maritime Museum)
1993.231

The Quakers were amongst the earliest opponents of slavery and the slave trade. Their nationwide network of groups provided a powerful weapon in the campaign against the trade.

167 (not illus.)
William Roscoe, after John Williamson (1751-1818), oil on canvas, (painted surface within oval)
428x360mm
NML (Walker Art Gallery)
6136

William Roscoe (1753-1831) is probably the best known of the supporters of abolition in Liverpool. A self-made man, he began his career as a lawyer and later moved into banking. He had wide literary and artistic interests and was a noted writer and collector. He wrote a long poem, 'The Wrongs of Africa', and many pamphlets in favour of abolition. Opinion in Liverpool was generally pro-slavery and like other abolitionists, Roscoe tended to work behind the scenes rather than openly declaring his views. He was the town's Member of Parliament in 1806-7 but this was not an issue in his election and he was not active in the debates which lead to abolition.

168 (illus. p. 84)
Patch box, with abolitionist motif, 'AM I NOT A MAN AND A BROTHER', Enamel on copper, South Staffordshire, circa 1790
48x39x26mm
NML (Walker Art Gallery)
1987.212.3

169 (illus. p. 86)
'African Hospitality', illustrating verse 'Dauntless they plunge amidst the vengeful waves, / And snatch from death the lovely sinking fair- / Their friendly efforts lo! each Briton saves / Perhaps their future Tyrants now they spare', engraved by J R Smith, King Street, Covent Garden London, after George Morland , 1 February 1791
640x803mm
NML (Merseyside Maritime Museum)
1991.389.1

170 (illus. p. 87)
'Slave Trade', illustrating verse 'Lo! the poor Captive with distraction wild / Views his dear Partner torn from his embrace !/ A different Captain buys his Wife and Child / What time can from his Soul such ills erase', engraved by J R Smith, King Street, Covent Garden, London, after George Morland, 1 February 1791
640x803mm
NML (Merseyside Maritime Museum)
1991.389.2.

171 (illus. p. 84)
One Penny Token, Obverse: chained slave kneeling in supplication, 'AM I NOT A MAN AND A BROTHER' Reverse: WHATSOEVER / YE WOULD THAT / MEN SHOULD DO / UNTO YOU, DO YE / EVEN SO TO / THEM', c1790
NML (World Museum Liverpool)
DH 235

172
Half-penny token, Obverse: chained slave kneeling in supplication, 'AM I NOT A MAN AND A BROTHER', Reverse: clasped hands, 'MAY SLAVERY & OPPRESSION CEASE THROUGHOUT THE WORLD'
NML (Walker Art Gallery)
68.219.151

173 (illus. p. 84)
Half-penny token Obverse: 'AM I NOT A MAN AND A BROTHER', Reverse: clasped hands, 'MAY SLAVERY & OPPRESSION CEASE THROUGHOUT THE WORLD'
NML (World Museum Liverpool)
69.109.411

174
Half-penny token, Obverse: 'AM I NOT A MAN AND A BROTHER', Reverse: 'WHATSOEVER YE WOULD THAT MEN SHOULD DO TO YOU, DO YE EVEN SO TO THEM'
NML (World Museum Liverpool)
N/N

These tokens were produced for The Society for the Suppression of the African Slave Trade, which was founded in 1787. They were issued between 1787 and the abolition of the trade in 1807.

174

176

179

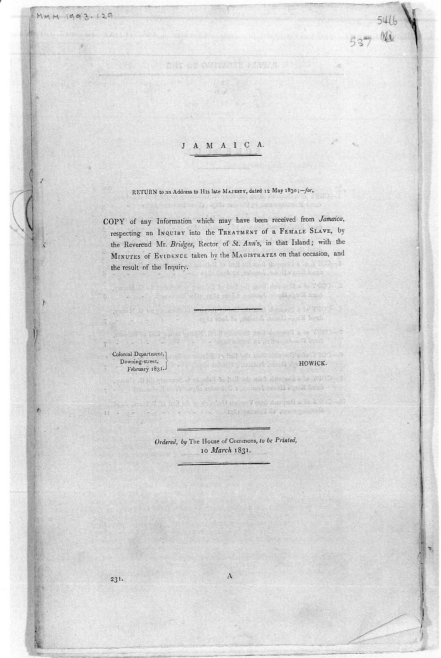

JAMAICA.

RETURN to an Address to His late MAJESTY, dated 12 May 1830;—*for,*

COPY of any Information which may have been received from *Jamaica,* respecting an INQUIRY into the TREATMENT of a FEMALE SLAVE, by the Reverend Mr. *Bridges,* Rector of *St. Ann's,* in that Island; with the MINUTES of EVIDENCE taken by the MAGISTRATES on that occasion, and the result of the Inquiry.

Colonial Department,
Downing-street,
February 1831.

HOWICK.

Ordered, by The House of Commons, *to be Printed,*
10 *March* 1831.

231.   A

175 (not illus.)
One Cent, Sierra Leone Company, Bronze, 1791,
Obverse: Lion, 'Sierra Leone Company, Africa',
Reverse: clasped hands, 'One Cent Piece 1791'
NML (World Museum Liverpool)
66.300.193

176
One Cent, Sierra Leone Company, Bronze, 1791,
Obverse: Lion, 'Sierra Leone Company, Africa',
Reverse: clasped hands, 'One Cent Piece 1791'
NML (World Museum Liverpool)
N/N

These coins were designed by Matthew Boulton and struck at his Soho Mint in Birmingham. They were produced for the Sierra Leone Company, which was responsible for the establishment of a colony of ex-slaves, who had fought for the British during the American War of Independence but who were not welcome in England.

177 (illus. p. 69)
Oval Epergne, Silver plate, by Pitts and Preedy, engraved with the arms of the Town of Liverpool and those of Machell of Penny Bridge, co. Lancaster, impaling Penny, inscribed 'This is one of two Pieces of Silver Plate presented to JAMES PENNY ESQr by The CORPORATION OF LIVERPOOL 1792.' A later inscription on the central bowl reads 'John Penny Machell Esquire, of Penny Bridge and Hollow Oak gave on 23rd October 1877 to Andrew Hay Wilson this piece of plate which was originally presented to their Grandfather James Penny by the Corporation of Liverpool.'
457mm high, 114oz, 1792
NML (Walker Art Gallery)
1973.278

This Epergne, was one of two pieces of plate, valued at £100, which were presented to James Penny in 1792 by the Liverpool Town Council in recognition of his support for the slave trade. He was a prominent Liverpool slave trader and regularly sent vessels to the West African coast and Angola. Penny gave evidence in the parliamentary enquiries into the trade and, with others, had been given the freedom of the borough in 1788 'for the very essential advantages derived to the trade of Liverpool from their evidence in support of the African slave trade, and for the public spirit they have manifested.'

178 (illus. p. 40)
25 Centimes, Silver, Haiti, Petion Republic, 1816,
Obverse: palm tree and trophy of arms and flags,
Reverse: '25c' in snake 'REPUBLIQUE D'HAYTI AN 13'

Haiti, the former French colony of St Domingue, was the first Caribbean island to achieve independence in 1804 after a long and bloody revolt which began in 1789. A separate republic under Alexander Petion, was declared in the south-west of the island in 1807.

179
Copy of information relating to an inquiry into the treatment of a female slave by Rev. Mr Bridges, Rector of St Ann's, Jamaica, printed 10 March 1831
350x215mm
NML (Merseyside Maritime Museum)

180 (illus. p. 89)
Plate, white china, printed in brown with abolitionist motifs and mottoes, early 19th century
225(dia) mm
NML (Walker Art Gallery)
54.124.5

181 (illus. p. 91)
Comport, white china, printed in brown with abolitionist motifs and mottoes, early 19th century
335x280x162mm
NML (Walker Art Gallery)
54.124.1

182 (illus. p. 88)
Small cup, white china, printed in green with tropical scene and overseer whipping a kneeling and chained slave, 'From Sun to Sun the Negro toils / No smiles reward his trusty care, / And when the indignant mind recoils, / His doom is whips and black despair', 19th century
75(dia)x68mm
NML (Walker Art Gallery)
54.171.486

183 (illus. p. 89)
Sugar bowl, ironstone, brown glazed inscribed in gilt lettering 'East Indies sugar Not Made By Slaves', c.1822-34
130(dia)x80mm
Norwich Castle Museum
37.934

184 (illus. p. 91)
Pair of figure groups, celebrating the end of slavery, porcelain, painted in enamel colours, Staffordshire, c.1830-40
178mm
NML (Walker Art Gallery)
1990.23

This pair depicts before and after emancipation. The before group follows a standard abolitionist motif. The after scene shows a freed slave with discarded irons and whip, standing before Britannia, identifiable by her helmet, shield and cornucopia.

185 (illus. p. 90)
Medal, by T. Halliday, Obverse: 'JUBILEE IN COMMEMORATION OF THE ABOLITION OF SLAVERY IN THE BRITISH COLONIES IN THE REIGN OF WILLIAM IV AUG 1 1834' and Reverse: freed man, woman and child, raising arms to heaven 'GIVE GLORY TO GOD', 1834
NML (World Museum Liverpool)
68.219.107

189

191

186 (illus. p. 90)
Medal, by J. Davis, Obverse: 'IN COMMEMORATION OF THE EXTINCTION OF COLONIAL SLAVERY THROUGHOUT THE BRITISH DOMINIONS IN THE REIGN OF WILLIAM THE IV AUGT 1 1834', Reverse: freed man standing in sunlight holding broken chains, 'THIS IS THE LORD'S DOING: IT IS MARVELLOUS IN OUR EYES PSALM 118 v.23 JUBILEE AUGT 1 1834', 1834
NML (World Museum Liverpool)
50.28.32

187 (illus. p. 90)
Medal, bronze, probably by T. Halliday, Obverse: William IV seated beneath canopy attended by 4 statesmen (Lords Grey, Russell, Brougham and Althorp) 'I ADVOCATE THE BILL AS A MEASURE OF HUMANITY', Reverse: Seven people hands joined dancing around a palm tree, 'SLAVERY ABOLISHED BY GREAT BRITAIN 1834', 1834
British Museum
M6222

188 (illus. p. 51)
Plate, white earthenware with blue transfer-printed scene of former slave family in front of cabin, 'FREEDOM FIRST OF AUGUST 1838', 265mm (dia)
NML (Merseyside Maritime Museum)
1992.128

Although slavery was abolished in the British colonies in 1834, former slaves were indentured as apprentices for a further four years before they were actually free. 1 August 1838 was regarded and celebrated as the first day of freedom.

189
Claim for compensation for loss of 103 slaves, plantation of Good Intent, 1 August 1834
335x207mm
Hull Museums
Box 10/3

Plantation owners in British colonies were compensated for the so-called loss of their slaves when the Emancipation Act was passed.

190
Promissory Note, for compensation for emancipated slaves, 6 April 1876
330x292mm
Museo de Puerto Rico

191
Electoral tally, United States of America, Obverse: 'MILLIONS FOR FREEDOM. NOT ONE PER CENT FOR SLAVERY', Reverse: an Eagle, 'SUCCESS TO REPUBLICAN PRINCIPLES', 18??
NML (World Museum Liverpool)
15.2.89.424

192 (illus. p. 65)
Token, United States of America, Obverse: 'AM I NOT A WOMAN AND A SISTER 1838', Reverse: a kneeling woman, 'UNITED STATES OF AMERICA LIBERTY 1838', 1838.
NML (World Museum Liverpool)
15.2.89.304

193 (illus. p. 75)
Manuscript Chart showing the tracks of a Royal Navy patrol vessel off the West African Coast, facsimile of chart by Edward Smith, 1843
National Maritime Museum, London
G241 6/9

This chart, which covers the area from Cape St. Bras to Little Fish Bay, probably shows the track of the Royal Navy patrol vessel *Bittern*. This 16-gun brig-rigged sloop was one of many British Naval ships on the so-called African Station charged to capture illegal slavers during the 1840s. The chart includes dates when slave ships were captured.

194 (not illus.)
'THE CELEBRATED PIRATICAL SLAVER L'ANTONIO, with other of the Black Craft lying in the Bonny River', engraved by T G Dutton after N. M. Condy, 1845.
455x535mm
NML (Merseyside Maritime Museum)
1992.143

195 (illus. p. 121)
Banshee, Builders' model, Scale 1:64, 1863
460x1040x100mm
NML (Merseyside Maritime Museum)
16.9.27.1

The paddle steamer *Banshee* was built in 1863 by Jones, Quiggin & Co. of Liverpool. She was the first of the so-called 'Blockade Runners' ordered by the Confederate States to beat the blockade imposed by the Federal Navy during the American Civil War. A number of ships were built for the Confederacy on Merseyside, where there was much support for their cause.

Select Bibliography

There is a huge literature on the subject of transatlantic slavery and the following is intended only as a basic guide to further reading.

Robin Blackburn, *The Making of New World Slavery: From the Baroque to the Modern 1492-1800*, London, 1997

Robin Blackburn, *The Overthrow of Colonial Slavery 1776-1848*, London, 1988

Barbara Bush, *Slave Women in Caribbean Society, 1650-1858*, London, 1990

Captive Passage: The Transatlantic Slave Trade and the Making of the Americas, Smithsonian Institution, 2002

Madge Dresser, *Slavery Obscured: The Social History of the Slave Trade in an English Provincial Port [Bristol]*, London, 2001

Melinda Elder, *The Slave Trade and the economic development of Lancaster*, Halifax, 1992

Peter Fryer, *Staying Power: The History of Black People in Britain*. London, 1984

David Hancock, *Citizens of the World: London Merchants and the Integration of the British Atlantic Community, 1735-1785*, Cambridge, 1995

Herbert S. Klein, *The Atlantic Slave Trade*, Cambridge, 1999

P. J. Marshall (ed.), *The Oxford History of the British Empire*, Volume II, The Eighteenth Century, Oxford, 1999

Patrick Manning, *Slavery and African Life*, Cambridge, 1990

Joseph C. Miller, *Way of Death: Merchant Capitalism and the Angolan slave trade, 1730-1830*, Madison, 1988

Kenneth Morgan, *Slavery, Atlantic Trade and the British Economy, 1660-1800*, Cambridge, 2000

Philip D. Morgan, *Slave Counterpoint: Black Culture in the Eighteenth-century Chesapeake and Lowcountry*, Chapel Hill, 1998

Philip D. Morgan & Sean Hawkins, *Black Experience and the Empire*, Oxford 2004

J.M. Postma, *The Dutch in the Atlantic Slave Trade 1600-1815*, Cambridge, 1990

Edward Reynolds, *Stand the Storm: A history of the Atlantic slave trade*, 1985

R. Stein, *The French Slave Trade in the Eighteenth Century: An Old Regime Business*, Madison, 1979

Hugh Thomas, *The Slave Trade: The History of the Atlantic Slave Trade, 1440-1870*, London, 1997

John Thornton, *Africa and Africans in the Making of the Atlantic World, 1400-1680*, Cambridge, 1992

James Walvin, *Black Ivory: A History of British Slavery*, London, 1992

Eric Williams, *Capitalism and Slavery*, North Carolina, 1944

Encyclopedias

Macmillan Encyclopedia of World Slavery, 2 vols, Paul Finkelmann & Joseph C Miller (eds.), New York, 1998

A Historical Guide to World Slavery, Seymour Drescher & Stanley L Engermann, Oxford, 1998

The Historical Encyclopedia of World Slavery, 2 vols, Julius P Rodriguez (ed.), Oxford, 1997

Documentary sources and memoirs

Donnan, E., *Documents Illustrative of the History of the Slave Trade to America*, 4 vols, Washington, 1930-35

Olaudah Equiano, *The Interesting Narrative and Other Writings*, Vincent Carretta (ed), London, 1995

Alexander Falconbridge, *An Account of the Slave Trade on the Coast of Africa*, New York, reprinted 1973

D. Hall, *In Miserable Slavery: Thomas Thistlewood in Jamaica, 1750-1786*, London, 1989

The History of Mary Prince, A West Indian Slave, related by herself, M. Ferguson, ed London, 1987

Harriet Jacobs, *Incidents in the Life of a slave girl*, Oxford, 1988

Peter Kitson & Debbie Lee, *Slavery, Abolition and Emancipation: Writings in the British Romantic Period*, 8 vols., London, 1999

B. Martin, & Martin Spurrell, *The Journal of A Slave Trader, John Newton, 1750-1754*, London, 1962

The Trans-Atlantic Slave Trade: A Database on CD-Rom, David Eltis, Stephen D. Behrendt, David Richardson & Herbert S. Klein, (editors) Cambridge, 1999

James Walvin, *An African's Life: Olaudah Equiano*, London, 1998

Photographic Credits

The Editor is grateful to David Flower, Senior Photographer, for photographing most of the NML objects for this catalogue and for copying and preparing all the other photography and to Joanne Howdle, Assistant Curator in the Maritime History department, for handling all the administrative work with such patience and efficiency. Credits refer to catalogue numbers.

American Museum of Natural History
(Courtesy of the Department of Library Services, photographs by D. Finnin) 127(neg.no.5173[3]), 128(5174[3]). 129(5175[2]), 133(5172[3])

American Numismatic Society 139

Biblioteca Medicea Laurenziana, Florence fig.1

Bibliothèque Nationale de France, Paris, fig.25

British Library figs.3, 7, 8, 10, 11, 14, 21, 24, 29

Board of Trustees of the National Museums Liverpool 1-9, 11-28, 30, 36, 38-45, 48-50, 54-61, 63-65, 67-75, 77, 82, 84-91, 93, 94, 96, 97, 99, 112-24, 126, 138, 147-55, 159, 162-82, 184-86, 188, 191, 192, 194, 195, figs.12, 13, 16, 18, 27, 28, 30-35

Chicago Historical Society (Courtesy of Decorative and Industrial Arts Collection) 140

Dapper Collection, Paris fig.22

J. L. Charmet, Paris, fig.26

Library of Congress figs.5, 6

Liverpool City Libraries fig.15

Mary Evans Picture Library figs.4, 23

Museum of History, Anthropology and Art of University of Puerto Rico 134-36, 190

Museum of Science and Industry in Manchester 160

National Maritime Museum
51-53, 62, 92, 100-11, 193 figs.2, 9

Norwich Castle Museum, Norfolk Museum Service 183

Science Museum 98

Tate and Lyle Sugars plc 145, 146

Texas Memorial Museum, University of Texas at Austin (division of History and Anthropology) 130, 131

Trustees of the British Museum
10, 29, 31-35, 46, 47, 78-81, 132, 187, fig.17

Walker Art Gallery/Bridgeman Art Library fig.20

Whitby Museum 125

Wilberforce Museum, Hull City
Museums and Art Galleries
137, 141-143, 189, fig.19

Index